ALA-APA Salary Survey

Librarian—Public and Academic

2008

Jenifer Grady and Denise M. Davis
Project Directors

ALA-APA Survey Report

American Library Association-Allied Professional Association:
the Organization for the Advancement of Library Employees

American Library Association, Office for Research and Statistics

ALA APA
the organization for the
advancement of library employees

OFFICE FOR
RESEARCH AND STATISTICS

ISBN 978-0-8389-8485-7

Printed in the United States of America

Acknowledgments

Thanks are due to the many respondents who completed the 2008 *Librarian Salary Survey* questionnaire. Without their cooperation, this report would not be possible. We are grateful for the responses from new participants as we continue to fulfill our goal to gather and report state level data. And we are indebted to the staff at larger public and academic libraries that participate every year without fail.

Association of Research Libraries (ARL) members have been willing to share their data with us for many years, as described in Appendix B. We thank Martha Kyrillidou, ARL Director for Statistics and Service Quality Programs, for her support and coordination of this aspect of the project.

The survey was conducted by The Management Association of Illinois, our consultant since 2006.

Kristy Williams, CCP, Manager of Compensation Services, executes the survey with professionalism and a continued commitment to improve the experience for participants, with the help of Jean Hannon, Coordinator of Compensation Services. The Association managed the mailings, processed the returns and analyzed the results. On behalf of the respondents, we thank The Association for providing so many methods for submitting salary data.

Finally, thanks are due to all in the library community who complete the survey, purchase the survey in print or by subscribing to the *Library Salary Database*, and use the survey for professional and personal research. We welcome back Angela Hanshaw, who formatted this edition, and appreciate Jamie Bragg's editorial assistance.

Table of Contents

Introduction

This is the fourth year that the American Library Association-Allied Professional Association: the Organization for Advancement of Library Employees (ALA-APA) has conducted a national survey of librarian salaries. The American Library Association (ALA) conducted a periodic survey of salaries for full-time professionals in academic and public libraries from 1982 to 2004. This year, the *ALA-APA Salary Survey: Librarian—Public and Academic*, which will heretofore be referred to as the *Librarian Salary Survey*, has one slight change to the title Librarian Who Does Not Supervise, which was previously Librarians Who Do Not Supervise. The change was made because the other titles are singular.

We continue to improve this survey to ensure that librarians, the people who hire them and interested others will have accurate data about the salaries paid in a particular position and working in a particular type of library. This survey included smaller public libraries (serving less than 10,000)—of our nation's 9,198 total public library systems, 59.4 percent serve populations less than 10,000. There are 3,653 academic libraries nationwide. The survey continues to gather and report salary data at the state-level as well as regionally.

The survey was conducted by the ALA-APA in consultation with the ALA Office for Research and Statistics (ORS). The Management Association of Illinois in Downers Grove, Illinois, prepared the web- and paper-based surveys and response sheet, answered respondent questions and performed the mailing, processing and computer analysis of the survey responses.

Details of the ALA-APA *Librarian Salary Survey*:

- It includes salaries for six positions:
  - Director/Dean/Chief Officer
  - Deputy/Associate/Assistant Director
  - Department Head/Branch Manager/Coordinator/Senior Manager
  - Manager/Supervisor of Support Staff
  - Librarian Who Does Not Supervise (previously: Librarians Who Do Not Supervise)
  - Beginning Librarian
- It was based on salaries paid to incumbents in positions as of February 1, 2008.

- It was based on a survey of **libraries**, not individual librarians.
- It was based on a survey of **public** and **academic** libraries only. Sources for salaries in other library types are given in Appendix D.
- It was based on a survey of libraries with at least **three staff members**. See Appendix B for more information.
- Data for the nation is stratified into **four geographic areas**, as well as by **state**: North Atlantic, Great Lakes & Plains, Southeast West & Southwest. See Appendix B for a list of states included in each region.
- It shows the **first quartile, median and third quartile** for salaries paid in each type/size of library in addition to the **mean** and **range** (minimum and maximum) for each position reported.

This annual salary survey periodically includes "Supplementary Questions" to gather information on an issue related to library personnel. For 2008, the questions regarded the availability of the following benefits to Full-Time Professional, Part-Time Professional, Full-Time Support and Part-Time Support Staff. This question is a five-year update for the question last asked in 2003 by the ALA Office for Research and Statistics—http://www.ala.org/ala/ors/reports/employeebenefits.cfm:

Please indicate (☒) below what benefits your library provides and which staff are eligible. Use your own definitions of full-time and part-time. Do not report benefits that are for the director only as determined by contract negotiations.

- Bereavement leave
- Child care
- Credit union
- Dental insurance
- Disability insurance
- Elder care
- Flexible spending plans
- Health insurance
- Life insurance
- Long-term care
- Pension

- Personal days
- Prescription benefits
- Professional memberships
- Retirement savings
- Sick leave
- Training & education
- Transportation subsidies
- Tuition reimbursement
- Vacation
- Vision insurance
- Other

Results of the supplemental questions and analyses of the data are fully reported separately in issues of the ALA-APA monthly newsletter, *Library Worklife: HR E-News for Today's Leaders*, http://www.ala-apa.org/newsletter/current.html, as well as on the ALA Office for Research and Statistics' Reports web site, http://www.ala.org/ala/ors/reports/reports.htm.

Results

The survey questionnaire was mailed to a stratified sample of 3,484 public and academic libraries, including a sample of the membership of the Association of Research Libraries (ARL). The samples were drawn from the National Center for Education Statistics (NCES) data files *Academic Libraries: 2006* and *Public Libraries in the United States: Fiscal Year 2005*.[1] Surveys were sent to a sample of 1,988 public and 1,496 academic libraries, using a proportional sampling procedure that took into account the size of the population in each group by state and geographic region and the expected response rate to the survey. Libraries received a letter sent January 21, 2008, directing them to the complete the survey by using a web site developed by The Management Association of Illinois.

By March 23, 2008, usable responses had been received from 1,010 libraries (609 public, 401 academic), 29 percent of those sampled. In 2007, usable responses were received from 834 libraries, a 24 percent response rate. The response rates since 2004 have fluctuated, lower since the sample size was increase to garner state-level data and in years when both the *ALA-APA Salary Survey: Librarian—Public and Academic (Librarian Salary Survey)* and *ALA-APA Salary Survey: Non-MLS—Public and Academic (Non-MLS Salary Survey)* were issued. In all years since 2004, the preferred minimum response rate of fifty percent has been elusive. See **Complicating Factors** in the **Discussion** section for more details.

The results of this survey are presented on the following pages in six sets of tables for public libraries and six sets of tables for academic libraries. Each set reflects salaries for each position title (see Appendix A for position descriptions). Association of Research Libraries (ARL) member data was included with University data for four positions.

- Director/Dean/Chief Officer—**includes ARL member data**
- Deputy/Associate/Assistant Director—**includes ARL member data**
- Department Head/Branch Manager/Coordinator/Senior Manager
- Manager/Supervisor of Support Staff
- Librarian Who Does Not Supervise—**includes ARL member data**
- Beginning Librarian—**includes ARL member data**

The tables present the number of positions for which salaries were reported (N), the minimum salary and the maximum salary (range), the mean (arithmetic average), first quartile, median and third quartile for each of the four U.S. Census regions and for states. This pattern is repeated for each type and size of library.

Caveats

Caveats should be observed in reading the tables. The intent of the survey is to collect and present a statistically valid report of regional- and state-level data for each position and library type. This was not possible with an overall response rate of 29 percent. Although we received at least one response from either a public or academic library in all states and the District of Columbia, separating those responses by library class and region reduced the significance of individual library responses.

Public library responses were received from all states except Arkansas, Delaware and the District of Columbia. Academic library responses were received from all 50 states and the District of Columbia.

Regional- and state-level salaries are reported in this survey for each position and by type of library, reporting despite the low response rate. Individual cases are not presented where there are so few libraries or library systems in a category or state that it would be possible to identify the individual salary, such as in a state where there is one Very Large public library and one Director. Standard association practices recommend that salaries only be reported when there are three or more responses.

These data are not representative, so use caution in reviewing them or re-using them in any way.

---

1. The academic libraries sample was drawn from the 2006 post-survey file provided by the U.S. Census Bureau solely for the purposes of this study.

Table 1 shows that Very Large public libraries had the highest response rate at 71 percent, an improvement of 10 percent over 2007. Medium public library response improved 12 points to 33 percent. The largest increase was in Large public libraries, which had a 28 percent response rate in 2007, compared with 49 percent this year. Very Small public libraries response rate dipped six points to 16 percent this year.

University response rates rose six points to 32 percent this year, and ARL member libraries had a 51 percent response rate, higher by 13 percent than in 2007. Response remains low for the second year for Two-Year college libraries (17 percent).

The higher the number of cases (N), the more reliable the results of the sample in providing a true picture of the total population. For Very Large public libraries (serving over 500,000), the response rate was sufficient for all regions. For Large public libraries (serving 100,000 to 499,999), the response rate was 30 percent or higher for Great Lakes & Plains and West & Southwest. For academic libraries, only the 4-Year college libraries in the West & Southwest had a sufficient response rate of 36 percent. Response rates are defined as the percentage of responses divided by the surveys sent by category. For example, thirty-six surveys were sent to Very Large public libraries in the West & Southwest region and twenty-three responded (23/36 = 64 percent).

Another caveat is that when the mean and the median are not close together, the mean is being influenced by some unusual values. When the mean is much higher than the median, there are several very high salaries. When the mean is much lower than the median, there are several very low salaries.

The following examples illustrate how to interpret the tables:

Public

On the first page of the public library tables, there were thirty-seven Director salaries reported by Very Small public libraries from the North Atlantic region. The minimum salary for the range reported for this position in this region was $31,912 and the maximum was $83,000. When all of the salaries were added together and the result was divided by the total number (37), the average or mean salary was $53,262. When all eighty-three of the Director salaries for all regions were arrayed from low to high, 25 percent fell below $41,383 (Q1), 50 percent fell below or at $49,661 (median) and 75 percent fell below $57,300 (Q3). The mean overall of $49,661 and median of $46,606 were $3,055 apart, meaning that Directors in the top 50 percent earned higher salaries that brought up the average by more than $3,000. State-level data for Directors of Very Small public libraries follows in the table below. A final set of cumulative Regional- and State-level data tables for Directors of all public libraries follows the five sets of tables for each size of public library.

Academic

On the first page of the academic library tables, there were thirteen Director salaries reported by Two-Year College Libraries from the North Atlantic region. The minimum salary for the range reported for this position in this region was $38,433 and the maximum was $93,901. When all of the salaries were added together and the result was divided by the total number (13), the average or mean salary was $75,674. When all eighty-

Table 1. Response Rate by Library Type

Library Type	Responding Libraries	Libraries Invited to Participate	Response Rate (%)
Very Small Public	88	541	16
Small Public	132	523	25
Medium Public	165	505	33
Large Public	166	337	49
Very Large Public	58	82	71
2-Year College	93	539	17
4-Year College	109	373	29
University & ARL	199	584	34
Total	1010	3484	29

nine of the Director salaries for all regions were arrayed from low to high, 25 percent of Director salaries fell below $60,000 (Q1), 50 percent fell below or at $68,646 (median) and 75 percent fell below $84,500 (Q3). The mean overall of $73,020 and median of $68,646 were $4,374 apart, meaning that Directors in the top 50 percent earned higher salaries that brought up the average by more than $4,000. State-level data for Directors of Two-Year college libraries follows in the table below. A final set of cumulative Regional- and State-level data tables for Directors of all academic libraries follows the three sets of tables for each type of academic library.

Public (Very Small to Very Large; Regional, State)

DIRECTOR/DEAN/CHIEF OFFICER

Chief officer of the library or library system.

Very Small Public Library (serving a population of less than 10,000)

Regional Data

	Min	Q1	Mean	Median	Q3	Max	N
North Atlantic	31,912	46,000	53,262	53,490	60,011	83,000	37
Great Lakes & Plains	28,975	39,000	45,399	45,000	50,000	78,000	37
Southeast	45,000	45,000	60,862	52,585	85,000	85,000	3
West & Southwest	29,120	35,000	48,138	44,275	46,280	89,875	6
ALL REGIONS	28,975	41,383	49,661	46,606	57,300	89,875	83

State Data

	Min	Q1	Mean	Median	Q3	Max	N
AK	43,597	43,597	43,597	43,597	43,597	43,597	1
AL	52,585	52,585	52,585	52,585	52,585	52,585	1
CO	89,875	89,875	89,875	89,875	89,875	89,875	1
CT	45,320	45,930	57,388	51,335	68,845	81,560	4
FL	85,000	85,000	85,000	85,000	85,000	85,000	1
IA	31,200	34,313	41,751	43,467	47,622	52,000	8
IL	42,080	45,760	57,545	53,650	72,128	78,000	6
IN	28,975	28,975	32,719	32,719	36,462	36,462	2
KS	39,089	39,089	47,799	41,383	62,924	62,924	3
MA	40,060	41,000	51,125	52,000	58,500	60,596	7
ME	33,720	46,606	51,753	52,495	60,200	65,000	6
MI	31,000	32,550	38,894	39,000	45,000	46,921	5
MT	29,120	29,120	29,120	29,120	29,120	29,120	1
NE	36,067	36,067	39,458	37,606	44,700	44,700	3
NH	31,912	35,173	44,243	43,003	55,000	57,368	6
NJ	65,000	65,000	65,000	65,000	65,000	65,000	1
NM	44,953	44,953	44,953	44,953	44,953	44,953	1
NY	43,680	45,000	56,461	46,000	64,625	83,000	5
OH	42,712	45,000	49,901	50,000	53,503	60,777	7
OR	35,000	35,000	35,000	35,000	35,000	35,000	1
RI	51,530	51,530	57,760	60,011	61,738	61,738	3
TN	45,000	45,000	45,000	45,000	45,000	45,000	1
UT	46,280	46,280	46,280	46,280	46,280	46,280	1
VT	52,085	56,526	57,344	56,617	58,198	63,294	5
WI	41,496	41,496	43,165	43,000	45,000	45,000	3

DIRECTOR/DEAN/CHIEF OFFICER—CONTINUED

Small Public Library (serving a population of 10,000 to 25,000)

Regional Data

	Min	Q1	Mean	Median	Q3	Max	N
North Atlantic	40,375	56,822	72,068	67,000	85,449	116,085	45
Great Lakes & Plains	40,976	54,000	63,283	60,488	74,373	104,988	57

Southeast	35,000	41,000	59,993	51,168	87,069	116,547	11
West & Southwest	49,350	61,200	76,049	73,380	87,877	117,420	11
ALL REGIONS	35,000	54,000	67,312	62,303	80,178	117,420	124

State Data

	Min	Q1	Mean	Median	Q3	Max	N
AK	70,000	70,000	70,000	70,000	70,000	70,000	1
AL	49,900	49,900	73,862	55,138	116,547	116,547	3
CA	73,380	73,380	94,320	92,160	117,420	117,420	3
CO	58,580	58,580	58,580	58,580	58,580	58,580	1
CT	66,000	66,000	66,000	66,000	66,000	66,000	1
FL	87,069	87,069	87,069	87,069	87,069	87,069	1
IA	40,976	57,283	62,287	62,000	75,000	76,175	5
IL	44,100	70,700	76,622	77,000	86,005	104,988	15
IN	41,845	42,436	50,592	50,108	59,000	59,571	5
KS	44,129	44,129	44,129	44,129	44,129	44,129	1
KY	38,600	38,600	40,200	41,000	41,000	41,000	3
LA	51,168	51,168	51,168	51,168	51,168	51,168	1
MA	45,598	54,000	63,214	62,165	75,000	80,356	6
ME	62,500	62,500	67,250	67,250	72,000	72,000	2
MI	44,000	45,462	56,754	58,116	61,283	73,548	6
MN	53,165	53,165	55,068	55,068	56,971	56,971	2
MO	54,000	54,000	54,000	54,000	54,000	54,000	1
ND	56,700	56,700	56,700	56,700	56,700	56,700	1
NE	68,600	68,600	68,600	68,600	68,600	68,600	1
NH	43,472	43,472	43,472	43,472	43,472	43,472	1
NJ	63,900	83,207	91,147	91,943	98,900	116,085	18
NY	40,375	54,856	61,737	60,255	60,485	95,200	9
OH	42,750	49,705	62,923	57,678	81,705	86,920	9
OR	72,000	72,000	72,000	72,000	72,000	72,000	1
PA	40,850	43,700	51,427	51,000	59,613	62,400	6
RI	50,000	50,000	57,470	57,470	64,939	64,939	2
SC	52,000	52,000	52,000	52,000	52,000	52,000	1
SD	50,325	50,325	56,265	56,265	62,205	62,205	2
TX	80,000	80,000	83,939	83,939	87,877	87,877	2
UT	61,200	61,200	61,200	61,200	61,200	61,200	1
VA	92,498	92,498	92,498	92,498	92,498	92,498	1
WI	53,870	57,908	60,057	61,621	63,076	63,924	9
WV	35,000	35,000	35,000	35,000	35,000	35,000	1
WY	49,350	49,350	61,960	61,960	74,570	74,570	2

DIRECTOR/DEAN/CHIEF OFFICER—CONTINUED
Medium Public Library (serving a population of 25,000 to 99,999)

Regional Data

	Min	Q1	Mean	Median	Q3	Max	N
North Atlantic	44,000	72,955	87,169	86,297	94,500	137,348	36
Great Lakes & Plains	43,000	64,500	79,362	78,500	93,449	127,000	61
Southeast	35,000	51,610	65,922	62,148	80,547	110,428	24

West & Southwest	43,692	73,056	87,712	92,000	101,652	147,929	41
ALL REGIONS	35,000	64,000	81,219	80,333	95,180	147,929	162

State Data

	Min	Q1	Mean	Median	Q3	Max	N
AK	60,590	60,590	60,590	60,590	60,590	60,590	1
AL	110,428	110,428	110,428	110,428	110,428	110,428	1
CA	73,092	95,000	107,458	108,696	124,000	147,929	13
CO	87,830	87,830	91,399	92,000	94,368	94,368	3
CT	131,250	131,250	131,250	131,250	131,250	131,250	1
FL	37,565	37,565	74,339	79,518	105,934	105,934	3
GA	51,670	57,412	62,018	64,077	66,625	68,249	4
IA	84,000	84,000	88,750	88,750	93,500	93,500	2
ID	61,460	61,460	66,413	66,413	71,365	71,365	2
IL	43,000	68,832	88,662	90,229	108,500	127,000	20
IN	56,431	60,268	74,487	73,242	82,742	101,000	6
KY	64,150	64,150	64,150	64,150	64,150	64,150	1
LA	35,000	35,000	64,138	56,455	100,958	100,958	3
MA	72,909	76,500	82,332	83,061	88,140	90,000	10
MD	112,000	112,000	112,000	112,000	112,000	112,000	1
ME	81,101	81,101	86,082	86,082	91,062	91,062	2
MI	46,592	54,000	79,924	90,099	95,180	103,572	6
MN	70,464	70,464	78,018	78,018	85,572	85,572	2
MO	48,000	48,000	58,274	59,872	66,950	66,950	3
NC	52,432	52,432	60,000	60,000	67,568	67,568	2
ND	85,290	85,290	85,290	85,290	85,290	85,290	1
NH	67,983	67,983	67,983	67,983	67,983	67,983	1
NJ	85,000	86,449	99,528	93,000	110,861	133,046	9
NV	94,000	94,000	94,000	94,000	94,000	94,000	1
NY	66,423	73,000	102,939	117,500	120,422	137,348	5
OH	55,000	64,500	76,096	68,058	85,218	123,053	11
OR	73,056	73,056	86,176	92,208	93,264	93,264	3
PA	44,000	47,250	57,597	60,732	62,000	70,870	6
RI	75,340	75,340	75,340	75,340	75,340	75,340	1
TN	37,916	37,916	37,916	37,916	37,916	37,916	1
TX	43,692	50,777	76,659	81,836	96,300	109,720	12
UT	84,854	84,854	84,854	84,854	84,854	84,854	1
VA	42,000	50,000	63,344	55,292	82,583	103,000	7
WA	82,225	82,225	93,936	99,288	100,296	100,296	3
WI	50,000	61,800	71,068	68,329	78,544	92,037	10
WV	61,142	61,142	71,359	71,359	81,576	81,576	2
WY	45,200	45,200	46,263	46,263	47,325	47,325	2

DIRECTOR/DEAN/CHIEF OFFICER—CONTINUED
Large Public Library (serving a population of 100,000 to 499,999)

Regional Data

	Min	Q1	Mean	Median	Q3	Max	N
North Atlantic	69,424	89,074	105,841	94,635	132,406	150,000	15
Great Lakes & Plains	72,864	94,080	102,992	103,532	110,481	139,526	45
Southeast	45,000	77,688	94,109	87,916	114,545	159,842	47
West & Southwest	54,434	98,763	119,068	115,282	137,631	197,952	52
ALL REGIONS	45,000	87,500	105,893	104,340	118,352	197,952	159

State Data

	Min	Q1	Mean	Median	Q3	Max	N
AL	91,258	91,258	108,258	108,258	125,258	125,258	2
AZ	81,551	86,824	98,306	96,676	109,788	118,322	4
CA	99,526	127,513	147,400	148,162	166,932	197,952	20
CO	79,100	98,000	104,167	101,765	107,000	134,972	5
FL	74,027	80,251	90,975	86,539	104,456	112,151	11
GA	56,900	56,900	77,450	77,450	98,000	98,000	2
IA	103,540	103,540	114,773	114,773	126,006	126,006	2
IL	83,824	91,912	106,204	109,413	120,497	122,168	4
IN	81,898	94,080	101,735	97,611	99,684	139,526	6
KS	106,090	106,090	110,088	110,088	114,085	114,085	2
KY	85,010	85,010	111,023	111,023	137,035	137,035	2
LA	45,000	45,000	57,294	57,294	69,587	69,587	2
MA	111,151	111,151	111,151	111,151	111,151	111,151	1
MD	106,000	111,000	122,414	124,203	133,828	135,250	4
MI	90,520	91,821	104,544	101,462	107,958	136,500	7
MN	80,617	84,094	95,610	95,821	108,930	109,079	7
MO	75,650	75,650	97,875	103,532	114,444	114,444	3
MS	74,263	74,532	79,155	79,178	83,778	84,000	4
NC	55,117	62,232	86,340	86,594	112,500	115,000	6
NE	105,034	105,034	111,905	111,905	118,776	118,776	2
NJ	87,000	89,989	109,038	94,620	138,000	150,000	6
NY	69,424	69,424	79,249	79,249	89,074	89,074	2
OH	72,864	96,281	106,158	110,241	119,800	123,760	8
OK	100,000	100,000	100,000	100,000	100,000	100,000	1
OR	54,434	54,434	84,925	96,000	104,340	104,340	3
PA	80,772	80,772	87,042	87,042	93,311	93,311	2
SC	80,000	98,556	112,475	109,434	114,545	159,842	5
TN	51,650	69,214	78,620	72,209	82,363	117,662	5
TX	58,685	90,000	95,164	93,399	106,840	126,560	9
UT	109,304	109,304	109,304	109,304	109,304	109,304	1
VA	85,675	114,397	115,526	117,050	123,370	128,904	8
WA	94,744	107,497	113,972	115,242	118,178	135,200	8
WI	84,989	89,987	95,483	95,705	100,980	105,535	4

2008 ALA-APA Librarian Salary Survey

Public (Very Small to Very Large; Regional, State)

DIRECTOR/DEAN/CHIEF OFFICER—CONTINUED
Very Large Public Library (serving a population of 500,000 or more)

Regional Data

	Min	Q1	Mean	Median	Q3	Max	N
North Atlantic	107,000	153,827	172,492	167,063	220,000	220,000	6
Great Lakes & Plains	114,062	121,688	135,899	133,900	147,000	162,847	5
Southeast	99,786	114,628	134,103	124,688	148,580	183,851	12
West & Southwest	82,014	124,979	142,434	141,276	156,811	202,446	32
ALL REGIONS	82,014	123,594	143,301	139,752	159,521	220,000	55

State Data

	Min	Q1	Mean	Median	Q3	Max	N
AZ	139,515	139,515	147,108	144,211	154,700	160,493	4
CA	101,976	124,300	152,175	144,396	200,573	202,446	11
CO	123,594	123,594	123,594	123,594	123,594	123,594	1
FL	113,922	115,333	144,919	136,551	183,304	183,851	6
GA	99,786	106,543	114,604	116,890	122,664	124,848	4
MD	153,827	153,827	162,651	157,132	176,993	176,993	3
MO	133,900	133,900	133,900	133,900	133,900	133,900	1
NY	107,000	107,000	182,333	220,000	220,000	220,000	3
OH	147,000	147,000	154,924	154,924	162,847	162,847	2
OK	147,324	147,324	153,423	153,423	159,521	159,521	2
TX	124,848	125,109	131,508	128,347	139,596	142,800	6
WA	139,752	139,752	157,252	154,101	177,902	177,902	3

DIRECTOR/DEAN/CHIEF OFFICER—CONTINUED
ALL PUBLIC LIBRARIES

Regional Data

	Min	Q1	Mean	Median	Q3	Max	N
North Atlantic	31,912	56,526	78,953	72,909	93,000	220,000	139
Great Lakes & Plains	28,975	54,000	75,328	72,128	95,180	162,847	205
Southeast	35,000	58,985	87,185	84,000	113,126	183,851	97
West & Southwest	29,120	83,672	108,951	106,670	135,200	202,446	142
ALL REGIONS	28,975	58,685	86,354	83,000	108,000	220,000	583

State Data

	Min	Q1	Mean	Median	Q3	Max	N
AK	43,597	43,597	58,062	60,590	70,000	70,000	3
AL	49,900	52,585	85,873	91,258	116,547	125,258	7
AZ	81,551	96,676	122,707	128,919	144,211	160,493	8
CA	73,092	109,402	134,082	132,877	157,320	202,446	47
CO	58,580	87,830	97,008	94,368	107,000	134,972	11
CT	45,320	46,540	71,133	61,065	81,560	131,250	6
FL	37,565	82,000	102,969	95,209	113,922	183,851	22
GA	51,670	63,154	86,139	83,125	113,300	124,848	10
IA	31,200	41,201	61,911	52,000	76,175	126,006	17
ID	61,460	61,460	66,413	66,413	71,365	71,365	2

IL	42,080	68,099	82,059	79,141	100,000	127,000	45
KS	39,089	41,383	67,950	53,527	106,090	114,085	6
LA	35,000	45,000	59,695	53,812	69,587	100,958	6
MA	40,060	55,665	69,651	73,871	83,275	111,151	24
MD	106,000	114,000	136,201	133,828	155,480	176,993	8
ME	33,720	51,500	61,718	61,350	72,000	91,062	10
MI	31,000	46,027	72,764	67,416	97,176	136,500	24
MN	53,165	70,464	85,040	85,572	103,328	109,079	11
MO	48,000	56,936	82,044	71,300	108,988	133,900	8
MS	74,263	74,532	79,155	79,178	83,778	84,000	4
NC	52,432	58,675	79,755	75,378	101,250	115,000	8
ND	56,700	56,700	70,995	70,995	85,290	85,290	2
NE	36,067	37,606	68,464	56,650	105,034	118,776	6
NH	31,912	37,437	47,114	44,889	56,184	67,983	8
NJ	63,900	85,000	95,754	92,793	102,004	150,000	34
NY	40,375	55,839	85,755	67,924	101,100	220,000	24
OH	42,712	54,600	78,697	68,058	96,315	162,847	37
OK	100,000	100,000	135,615	147,324	159,521	159,521	3
PA	40,850	47,000	59,159	59,655	62,400	93,311	14
RI	50,000	51,530	60,593	60,875	64,939	75,340	6
SC	52,000	80,000	102,396	103,995	114,545	159,842	6
SD	50,325	50,325	56,265	56,265	62,205	62,205	2
TN	37,916	45,000	68,002	69,214	82,363	117,662	7
TX	43,692	80,000	94,252	93,000	118,352	142,800	29
VT	52,085	56,526	57,344	56,617	58,198	63,294	5
WA	82,225	100,296	118,953	115,242	135,200	177,902	14
WV	35,000	35,000	59,239	61,142	81,576	81,576	3
WY	45,200	46,263	54,111	48,338	61,960	74,570	4

DEPUTY/ASSOCIATE/ASSISTANT DIRECTOR

Persons who report to the Director and manage major aspects of the library operation (e.g., technical services, public services, collection development, systems/automation).
Very Small Public Library (serving a population of less than 10,000)

Regional Data

	Min	Q1	Mean	Median	Q3	Max	N
North Atlantic	26,719	38,293	42,829	40,640	53,867	54,624	5
Great Lakes & Plains	28,000	28,000	32,199	34,278	34,320	34,320	3
ALL REGIONS	26,719	31,139	38,843	36,307	47,254	54,624	8

State Data

	Min	Q1	Mean	Median	Q3	Max	N
IA	34,320	34,320	34,320	34,320	34,320	34,320	1
MA	26,719	26,719	40,672	40,672	54,624	54,624	2
ME	40,640	40,640	40,640	40,640	40,640	40,640	1
NY	53,867	53,867	53,867	53,867	53,867	53,867	1
OH	34,278	34,278	34,278	34,278	34,278	34,278	1
VT	38,293	38,293	38,293	38,293	38,293	38,293	1
WI	28,000	28,000	28,000	28,000	28,000	28,000	1

DEPUTY/ASSOCIATE/ASSISTANT DIRECTOR—CONTINUED
Small Public Library (serving a population of 10,000 to 25,000)

Regional Data

	Min	Q1	Mean	Median	Q3	Max	N
North Atlantic	30,992	41,600	55,268	58,000	63,696	87,715	21
Great Lakes & Plains	30,000	38,202	46,503	46,800	53,337	69,113	25
Southeast	47,144	47,144	48,156	47,466	49,858	49,858	3
West & Southwest	39,208	40,857	47,166	45,253	53,475	58,950	4
ALL REGIONS	30,000	40,768	50,120	48,000	59,000	87,715	53

State Data

	Min	Q1	Mean	Median	Q3	Max	N
AK	42,506	42,506	42,506	42,506	42,506	42,506	1
AL	47,144	47,144	47,144	47,144	47,144	47,144	1
CO	39,208	39,208	43,604	43,604	48,000	48,000	2
IA	43,000	43,000	52,542	52,542	62,083	62,083	2
IL	50,000	53,337	55,327	53,337	59,257	60,702	5
IN	30,000	30,700	37,227	32,926	40,768	57,731	7
MA	30,992	40,800	46,879	45,000	58,000	59,602	5
ME	34,860	34,860	38,787	40,060	41,440	41,440	3
MI	47,840	47,840	47,840	47,840	47,840	47,840	1
NJ	48,000	59,000	64,512	61,848	70,452	87,715	10
NY	69,600	69,600	69,600	69,600	69,600	69,600	1
OH	33,072	39,000	48,385	46,800	57,500	69,113	7
PA	41,600	41,600	47,573	47,573	53,546	53,546	2
SD	38,202	38,202	38,202	38,202	38,202	38,202	1
VA	47,466	47,466	48,662	48,662	49,858	49,858	2
WI	46,551	46,551	47,773	47,773	48,994	48,994	2
WY	58,950	58,950	58,950	58,950	58,950	58,950	1

DEPUTY/ASSOCIATE/ASSISTANT DIRECTOR—CONTINUED
Medium Public Library (serving a population of 25,000 to 99,999)

Regional Data

	Min	Q1	Mean	Median	Q3	Max	N
North Atlantic	30,000	54,876	65,809	61,951	77,987	110,176	27
Great Lakes & Plains	28,589	43,035	56,268	52,550	70,074	89,800	62
Southeast	32,401	39,291	58,868	61,320	70,034	89,561	15
West & Southwest	38,856	56,785	70,779	68,952	80,110	111,800	27
ALL REGIONS	28,589	45,840	61,523	61,214	74,375	111,800	131

State Data

	Min	Q1	Mean	Median	Q3	Max	N
AK	49,088	49,088	49,088	49,088	49,088	49,088	1
AL	78,520	78,520	80,090	80,090	81,660	81,660	2
CA	75,005	82,202	94,067	95,388	105,984	111,800	7
CO	65,794	65,794	72,952	72,952	80,110	80,110	2
CT	110,176	110,176	110,176	110,176	110,176	110,176	1

FL	57,200	57,200	63,765	64,060	70,034	70,034	3
GA	60,896	60,896	62,354	62,354	63,812	63,812	2
IA	38,376	48,433	61,312	61,464	74,192	83,946	4
ID	62,941	62,941	62,941	62,941	62,941	62,941	1
IL	31,990	44,628	65,619	72,735	80,300	89,800	17
IN	28,589	39,065	48,182	46,371	58,000	70,000	14
KY	36,250	36,250	36,250	36,250	36,250	36,250	1
LA	45,840	45,840	55,082	55,082	64,324	64,324	2
MA	50,635	57,887	60,524	60,922	64,859	68,810	10
MD	83,806	83,806	83,806	83,806	83,806	83,806	1
ME	52,583	52,583	52,583	52,583	52,583	52,583	1
MI	47,569	62,092	67,555	72,866	75,169	80,080	5
MN	40,726	43,971	48,000	47,711	51,653	55,938	5
NC	37,844	37,844	37,844	37,844	37,844	37,844	1
ND	70,074	70,074	70,074	70,074	70,074	70,074	1
NH	55,575	55,575	55,575	55,575	55,575	55,575	1
NJ	67,868	75,400	79,322	77,987	84,660	90,697	5
NV	65,000	65,000	65,000	65,000	65,000	65,000	1
NY	69,000	69,000	86,102	86,758	102,549	102,549	3
OH	35,300	43,035	49,174	44,591	50,565	78,769	9
OR	38,856	38,856	51,744	51,744	64,632	64,632	2
PA	30,000	32,500	39,339	36,241	46,179	54,876	4
RI	57,203	57,203	57,203	57,203	57,203	57,203	1
TN	32,401	32,401	32,401	32,401	32,401	32,401	1
TX	39,000	53,571	61,847	63,393	72,842	78,882	6
UT	54,868	54,868	54,868	54,868	54,868	54,868	1
VA	89,561	89,561	89,561	89,561	89,561	89,561	1
WA	50,963	61,388	66,701	67,386	73,580	79,500	6
WI	40,000	44,098	51,843	49,420	56,600	74,375	7
WV	39,291	39,291	50,306	50,306	61,320	61,320	2

DEPUTY/ASSOCIATE/ASSISTANT DIRECTOR—CONTINUED
Large Public Library (serving a population of 100,000 to 499,999)

Regional Data

	Min	Q1	Mean	Median	Q3	Max	N
North Atlantic	57,027	71,389	77,816	77,454	82,782	100,000	20
Great Lakes & Plains	33,883	60,633	71,428	72,758	83,824	102,585	71
Southeast	37,361	54,914	65,224	62,590	74,000	110,756	70
West & Southwest	36,171	73,601	83,394	83,415	94,000	157,872	70
ALL REGIONS	33,883	60,453	73,727	74,544	85,386	157,872	231

State Data

	Min	Q1	Mean	Median	Q3	Max	N
AL	76,845	76,845	89,485	93,475	98,134	98,134	3
AZ	68,155	69,424	81,793	86,970	86,970	97,448	5
CA	75,686	87,131	100,046	98,040	105,804	157,872	23
CO	54,497	58,718	72,749	71,065	79,000	102,150	6
FL	48,880	57,720	63,185	60,840	69,132	75,842	13

	Min	Q1	Mean	Median	Q3	Max	N
GA	69,312	69,312	69,312	69,312	69,312	69,312	1
IA	85,150	85,150	89,248	89,248	93,345	93,345	2
IL	74,544	76,581	85,383	83,824	92,888	99,080	5
IN	66,955	72,758	78,351	76,837	80,704	102,585	10
KS	59,207	67,074	71,001	69,386	71,948	89,003	6
KY	54,371	54,486	65,035	61,485	75,585	82,800	4
LA	40,000	41,850	48,038	47,184	54,225	57,782	4
MA	90,933	90,933	90,933	90,933	90,933	90,933	1
MD	74,200	77,825	84,527	78,705	97,726	100,000	6
MI	42,078	63,446	72,861	80,238	82,850	87,745	8
MN	33,883	47,904	59,756	59,115	72,778	84,456	12
MO	38,355	44,926	65,539	68,830	81,827	90,468	6
MS	46,300	48,950	54,367	55,050	59,784	61,067	4
MT	77,293	77,293	77,293	77,293	77,293	77,293	1
NC	37,361	41,139	53,743	53,590	60,000	78,000	9
NE	67,363	67,363	77,136	77,136	86,908	86,908	2
NJ	57,027	66,236	74,488	73,722	82,782	93,396	8
NV	94,000	94,000	94,523	94,523	95,046	95,046	2
NY	77,340	77,340	77,340	77,340	77,340	77,340	1
OH	45,365	54,080	69,691	65,634	87,836	99,598	14
OK	77,232	77,232	78,390	78,390	79,548	79,548	2
OR	36,171	36,171	53,612	40,664	84,000	84,000	3
PA	59,000	65,294	71,244	74,205	77,195	77,568	4
SC	46,356	56,565	64,956	62,064	69,696	110,350	16
TN	52,046	52,046	64,657	65,225	76,701	76,701	3
TX	44,073	60,437	68,569	71,041	77,216	84,522	12
UT	85,218	86,081	87,672	87,849	89,263	89,772	4
VA	59,149	66,680	78,448	75,615	85,398	110,756	13
WA	56,724	72,465	77,800	79,951	82,743	94,464	12
WI	65,770	69,014	72,225	70,759	72,046	85,000	6

DEPUTY/ASSOCIATE/ASSISTANT DIRECTOR—CONTINUED

Very Large Public Library (serving a population of 500,000 or more)

Regional Data

	Min	Q1	Mean	Median	Q3	Max	N
North Atlantic	57,920	74,880	101,670	100,000	121,550	176,800	25
Great Lakes & Plains	65,603	82,221	99,737	100,760	119,511	132,291	12
Southeast	59,405	72,738	93,270	92,127	105,082	138,569	35
West & Southwest	49,472	71,712	92,261	90,334	107,779	162,787	67
ALL REGIONS	49,472	73,743	94,853	92,609	109,307	176,800	139

State Data

	Min	Q1	Mean	Median	Q3	Max	N
AZ	90,334	99,385	103,733	105,685	110,531	110,781	6
CA	68,640	79,950	113,648	111,902	151,678	162,787	15
CO	78,874	78,874	86,362	83,304	96,907	96,907	3
FL	68,948	89,184	98,522	94,832	105,435	138,569	22
GA	79,482	85,688	91,891	88,206	101,220	104,860	5

HI	58,001	67,524	76,217	80,358	85,008	86,052	6
IN	76,896	77,665	89,212	88,524	100,760	102,906	4
KY	59,405	63,752	67,409	67,818	72,738	72,925	6
MD	84,358	88,664	106,429	108,716	122,001	127,197	7
MO	86,318	86,318	103,965	103,965	121,612	121,612	2
NM	58,074	58,074	61,059	61,059	64,043	64,043	2
NV	128,814	128,814	128,814	128,814	128,814	128,814	1
NY	57,920	72,609	99,820	91,274	121,550	176,800	18
OH	65,603	84,708	107,162	115,377	129,616	132,291	4
OK	71,712	78,168	86,228	82,344	100,194	102,606	6
OR	92,609	92,609	96,967	94,326	103,967	103,967	3
TX	49,472	54,255	72,346	66,681	88,938	107,664	16
UT	82,632	82,632	85,712	83,232	91,272	91,272	3
VA	111,866	111,866	116,523	116,523	121,181	121,181	2
WA	103,056	107,779	110,684	110,873	112,694	118,829	6
WI	86,008	86,008	101,709	101,709	117,409	117,409	2

DEPUTY/ASSOCIATE/ASSISTANT DIRECTOR—CONTINUED
ALL PUBLIC LIBRARIES

Regional Data

	Min	Q1	Mean	Median	Q3	Max	N
North Atlantic	26,719	57,203	73,976	70,517	85,847	176,800	98
Great Lakes & Plains	28,000	45,427	63,677	62,296	78,769	132,291	173
Southeast	32,401	57,720	72,013	67,309	85,688	138,569	123
West & Southwest	36,171	68,318	84,040	82,644	98,022	162,787	168
ALL REGIONS	26,719	55,938	73,385	71,115	87,131	176,800	562

State Data

	Min	Q1	Mean	Median	Q3	Max	N
AK	42,506	42,506	45,797	45,797	49,088	49,088	2
AL	47,144	76,845	79,296	80,090	93,475	98,134	6
AZ	68,155	86,970	93,761	97,448	109,179	110,781	11
CA	68,640	87,131	103,650	98,040	113,028	162,787	45
CO	39,208	58,718	71,438	71,681	80,110	102,150	13
CT	110,176	110,176	110,176	110,176	110,176	110,176	1
FL	48,880	66,685	83,689	74,044	101,234	138,569	38
GA	60,896	66,562	81,685	82,585	94,713	104,860	8
HI	58,001	67,524	76,217	80,358	85,008	86,052	6
IA	34,320	43,000	62,572	62,083	83,946	93,345	9
ID	62,941	62,941	62,941	62,941	62,941	62,941	1
IL	31,990	53,337	67,373	72,735	83,824	99,080	27
IN	28,589	39,065	59,300	58,000	76,896	102,906	35
KS	59,207	67,074	71,001	69,386	71,948	89,003	6
KY	36,250	54,600	63,713	66,206	72,738	82,800	11
LA	40,000	43,700	50,386	48,254	57,782	64,324	6
MA	26,719	50,635	56,217	58,801	61,951	90,933	18
MD	74,200	79,500	95,426	93,195	108,716	127,197	14
ME	34,860	40,060	41,917	40,640	41,440	52,583	5

MI	42,078	52,894	69,179	74,584	80,416	87,745	14
MN	33,883	47,093	56,299	53,190	62,059	84,456	17
MO	38,355	52,780	75,146	79,427	88,393	121,612	8
MS	46,300	48,950	54,367	55,050	59,784	61,067	4
MT	77,293	77,293	77,293	77,293	77,293	77,293	1
NC	37,361	38,293	52,153	49,989	60,000	78,000	10
ND	70,074	70,074	70,074	70,074	70,074	70,074	1
NE	67,363	67,363	77,136	77,136	86,908	86,908	2
NH	55,575	55,575	55,575	55,575	55,575	55,575	1
NJ	48,000	60,000	71,202	70,582	80,936	93,396	23
NM	58,074	58,074	61,059	61,059	64,043	64,043	2
NV	65,000	79,500	95,715	94,523	111,930	128,814	4
NY	53,867	70,309	93,995	82,124	112,050	176,800	24
OH	33,072	44,591	63,424	54,444	82,792	132,291	35
OK	71,712	77,700	84,268	80,580	91,635	102,606	8
OR	36,171	39,760	69,403	74,316	93,467	103,967	8
PA	30,000	37,481	53,748	54,211	71,587	77,568	10
RI	57,203	57,203	57,203	57,203	57,203	57,203	1
SC	46,356	56,565	64,956	62,064	69,696	110,350	16
SD	38,202	38,202	38,202	38,202	38,202	38,202	1
TN	32,401	42,224	56,593	58,636	70,963	76,701	4
TX	39,000	55,503	69,160	68,282	78,882	107,664	34
UT	54,868	82,932	82,837	86,081	89,263	91,272	8
VA	47,466	66,104	79,986	77,828	94,121	121,181	18
VT	38,293	38,293	38,293	38,293	38,293	38,293	1
WA	50,963	69,594	83,246	80,320	98,760	118,829	24
WI	28,000	46,551	62,401	61,185	72,046	117,409	18
WV	39,291	39,291	50,306	50,306	61,320	61,320	2
WY	58,950	58,950	58,950	58,950	58,950	58,950	1

DEPARTMENT HEAD/BRANCH MANAGER/COORDINATOR

Persons who supervise one or more professional librarians.
Very Small Public Library (serving a population of less than 10,000)

Regional Data

	Min	Q1	Mean	Median	Q3	Max	N
North Atlantic	36,321	37,214	43,723	40,000	49,245	61,527	7
Great Lakes & Plains	37,564	40,508	48,063	49,226	55,618	56,235	4
Southeast	45,000	45,000	45,000	45,000	45,000	45,000	1
ALL REGIONS	36,321	38,160	45,276	43,226	52,123	61,527	12

State Data

	Min	Q1	Mean	Median	Q3	Max	N
CT	37,214	37,214	47,247	43,000	61,527	61,527	3
FL	45,000	45,000	45,000	45,000	45,000	45,000	1
IL	55,000	55,000	55,618	55,618	56,235	56,235	2
MA	40,000	40,000	40,000	40,000	40,000	40,000	1
ME	38,755	38,755	38,755	38,755	38,755	38,755	1
NY	36,321	36,321	42,783	42,783	49,245	49,245	2
OH	37,564	37,564	40,508	40,508	43,451	43,451	2

DEPARTMENT HEAD/BRANCH MANAGER/COORDINATOR—CONTINUED

Small Public Library (serving a population of 10,000 to 25,000)

Regional Data

	Min	Q1	Mean	Median	Q3	Max	N
North Atlantic	33,009	45,767	53,314	51,488	57,976	100,109	30
Great Lakes & Plains	27,015	38,935	45,272	44,024	49,459	85,686	40
Southeast	40,601	40,601	62,336	69,706	76,700	76,700	3
West & Southwest	39,440	41,316	53,388	51,032	65,460	72,048	4
ALL REGIONS	27,015	40,601	49,491	47,706	54,971	100,109	77

State Data

	Min	Q1	Mean	Median	Q3	Max	N
AL	40,601	40,601	62,336	69,706	76,700	76,700	3
CA	58,872	58,872	65,460	65,460	72,048	72,048	2
CO	39,440	39,440	41,316	41,316	43,192	43,192	2
IL	35,100	42,000	49,329	47,500	50,700	85,686	25
IN	39,869	39,869	39,869	39,869	39,869	39,869	1
MA	56,000	56,000	57,500	57,500	59,000	59,000	2
ME	33,009	33,009	41,685	45,767	46,278	46,278	3
MI	32,000	32,965	38,764	34,645	44,564	53,768	4
NJ	38,490	48,415	58,073	54,152	61,665	100,109	16
NY	42,500	49,121	52,065	54,300	56,427	57,976	5
OH	29,557	30,462	38,617	33,699	46,772	57,512	4
PA	34,200	34,200	38,484	38,484	42,768	42,768	2
RI	43,243	43,243	46,448	46,448	49,652	49,652	2
SD	27,015	27,015	27,015	27,015	27,015	27,015	2
WI	40,123	41,080	43,555	43,951	46,031	46,197	4

DEPARTMENT HEAD/BRANCH MANAGER/COORDINATOR—CONTINUED

Medium Public Library (serving a population of 25,000 to 99,999)

Regional Data

	Min	Q1	Mean	Median	Q3	Max	N
North Atlantic	34,089	50,050	58,167	55,420	62,711	91,456	65
Great Lakes & Plains	25,000	45,331	54,336	52,560	62,159	85,200	100
Southeast	26,542	40,101	51,505	47,715	62,489	82,701	31
West & Southwest	34,476	51,012	59,035	55,370	69,264	82,440	43
ALL REGIONS	25,000	47,503	55,856	54,413	62,866	91,456	239

State Data

	Min	Q1	Mean	Median	Q3	Max	N
AK	44,928	44,928	44,928	44,928	44,928	44,928	1
AL	61,173	61,173	73,445	76,461	82,701	82,701	3
CA	41,510	62,566	68,716	71,724	78,324	82,440	15
CO	55,016	58,771	61,760	63,201	64,750	65,622	4
CT	71,823	71,823	80,363	80,111	89,156	89,156	3
FL	46,384	46,925	55,224	47,715	61,734	73,362	5
GA	46,350	46,350	57,141	55,074	70,000	70,000	3

IA	53,309	53,309	53,309	53,309	53,309	53,309	1
ID	51,002	51,002	51,002	51,002	51,002	51,002	1
IL	36,242	48,465	58,431	56,388	67,295	85,200	44
IN	37,202	41,021	47,606	49,566	52,083	58,240	15
KY	36,250	36,250	36,250	36,250	36,250	36,250	1
LA	45,936	45,936	45,936	45,936	45,936	45,936	1
MA	44,830	47,620	52,171	51,903	56,183	63,212	16
MD	68,650	68,650	68,650	68,650	68,650	68,650	2
ME	52,583	52,583	56,749	55,361	62,303	62,303	3
MI	47,771	52,476	58,668	59,985	63,700	69,118	10
MN	50,080	50,080	55,330	51,653	64,257	64,257	3
MO	43,780	43,780	43,780	43,780	43,780	43,780	1
NC	26,542	26,542	26,542	26,542	26,542	26,542	1
ND	52,325	52,325	52,325	52,325	52,325	52,325	1
NH	43,875	43,875	43,875	43,875	43,875	43,875	1
NJ	49,800	54,500	61,606	57,467	69,790	87,017	21
NV	53,000	53,000	53,000	53,000	53,000	53,000	1
NY	45,000	55,884	66,083	61,620	79,927	91,456	10
OH	25,000	43,125	47,974	48,331	53,801	64,729	16
OR	34,476	42,744	50,061	52,512	57,378	60,744	4
PA	34,089	39,644	43,556	42,579	48,609	52,699	8
RI	50,585	50,585	50,585	50,585	50,585	50,585	1
TN	26,936	26,936	26,936	26,936	26,936	26,936	1
TX	40,837	50,701	54,929	54,413	57,200	70,344	15
VA	28,000	57,585	55,885	59,105	64,701	70,245	9
WA	46,897	46,897	46,897	46,897	46,897	46,897	1
WI	36,500	42,786	53,209	56,878	62,132	65,677	9
WV	38,017	39,000	41,450	40,500	41,644	49,918	7
WY	40,699	40,699	40,699	40,699	40,699	40,699	1

DEPARTMENT HEAD/BRANCH MANAGER/COORDINATOR—CONTINUED
Large Public Library (serving a population of 100,000 to 499,999)

Regional Data

	Min	Q1	Mean	Median	Q3	Max	N
North Atlantic	42,287	54,097	60,999	59,037	68,587	87,911	104
Great Lakes & Plains	33,883	49,283	57,783	57,642	64,935	87,235	272
Southeast	27,000	46,899	55,608	53,301	62,443	105,485	252
West & Southwest	34,865	52,166	62,697	61,747	70,878	98,052	198
ALL REGIONS	27,000	49,504	58,702	57,565	66,331	105,485	826

State Data

	Min	Q1	Mean	Median	Q3	Max	N
AL	40,810	49,538	57,844	55,738	63,444	84,760	20
AZ	52,527	66,683	70,579	68,484	75,982	88,213	13
CA	49,908	64,752	73,624	71,859	80,827	98,052	62
CO	47,112	49,504	57,001	57,572	64,414	67,914	18
FL	39,144	46,243	55,713	53,209	62,287	101,586	62
GA	27,000	37,613	50,303	53,749	62,993	66,712	4

IA	60,911	66,640	72,330	72,482	78,180	83,130	8
IL	44,822	53,102	62,730	59,617	71,701	87,235	22
IN	39,000	46,155	53,242	52,333	60,237	71,115	62
KS	46,192	50,069	57,495	57,166	62,191	76,190	16
KY	41,995	46,946	54,816	54,579	62,322	67,315	18
LA	31,500	31,500	32,500	32,000	34,000	34,000	3
MA	42,861	51,826	57,575	57,906	62,441	72,512	6
MD	46,876	54,036	63,962	65,961	72,419	82,213	26
MI	41,142	48,614	55,808	53,778	61,370	80,208	23
MN	33,883	51,903	60,756	59,269	69,760	83,758	25
MO	43,890	52,749	61,546	61,000	69,103	84,063	29
MS	31,400	42,000	48,191	47,244	53,558	66,389	11
MT	56,222	56,222	56,222	56,222	56,222	56,222	1
NC	38,293	42,063	52,311	48,402	58,338	84,371	18
NE	44,247	52,446	57,006	60,189	61,621	68,695	9
NJ	42,287	53,648	60,207	58,781	68,060	87,911	62
NV	54,017	54,017	72,960	78,568	86,296	86,296	3
NY	54,687	55,385	56,387	56,685	57,388	57,490	4
OH	37,386	49,416	56,593	56,797	63,925	78,229	73
OK	39,132	40,308	46,426	44,052	55,788	57,456	7
OR	35,694	39,012	53,907	53,889	68,802	72,156	4
PA	58,567	58,858	62,853	59,423	69,378	71,470	6
SC	40,170	45,572	54,637	52,145	62,536	82,056	47
TN	32,920	47,069	54,478	53,486	65,702	73,274	14
TX	34,865	44,156	50,184	49,570	54,873	68,745	42
UT	48,817	52,332	60,158	62,545	65,874	69,721	13
VA	43,050	51,527	60,264	57,240	64,759	105,485	55
WA	45,681	56,403	62,866	61,633	69,369	85,140	35
WI	50,041	55,120	61,126	64,948	65,520	70,000	5

DEPARTMENT HEAD/BRANCH MANAGER/COORDINATOR—CONTINUED

Very Large Public Library (serving a population of 500,000 or more)

Regional Data

	Min	Q1	Mean	Median	Q3	Max	N
North Atlantic	42,759	53,715	63,648	59,624	69,566	122,001	254
Great Lakes & Plains	40,590	49,774	60,431	58,660	67,333	109,650	141
Southeast	38,733	51,813	63,213	60,532	71,922	106,782	307
West & Southwest	40,248	54,072	66,897	63,627	75,948	140,209	433
ALL REGIONS	38,733	53,038	64,370	61,020	71,891	140,209	1,135

State Data

	Min	Q1	Mean	Median	Q3	Max	N
AZ	49,643	60,426	68,774	66,144	76,481	110,651	47
CA	50,752	63,627	79,760	73,657	88,986	140,209	82
CO	66,144	66,467	68,365	67,392	70,263	72,530	4
FL	39,444	50,899	62,828	59,001	72,405	106,782	181
GA	38,733	54,908	61,161	60,738	68,688	81,876	54
HI	43,824	51,300	64,797	62,424	75,948	100,000	17

IN	40,590	43,966	50,847	45,676	54,870	74,270	29
KY	44,674	47,549	52,805	51,179	57,283	64,958	14
MD	43,687	61,131	74,234	71,997	87,513	122,001	72
MO	44,782	49,951	55,356	54,944	60,654	66,685	25
NM	46,280	50,898	57,123	56,400	62,213	71,843	10
NV	52,270	64,875	77,180	74,402	80,496	123,864	32
NY	42,759	52,926	59,460	57,665	63,336	98,870	182
OH	44,221	54,331	64,617	62,390	71,864	109,650	74
OK	40,248	50,964	58,335	58,284	64,522	85,200	25
OR	49,519	62,457	69,762	64,964	77,569	94,326	14
TX	42,612	49,440	56,324	53,123	61,440	79,439	138
UT	45,168	50,424	57,481	57,288	61,824	71,496	21
VA	45,059	57,342	68,839	68,751	79,611	104,597	58
WA	56,139	67,127	78,202	77,377	88,725	103,524	43
WI	55,180	58,658	67,738	64,293	74,921	91,200	13

DEPARTMENT HEAD/BRANCH MANAGER/COORDINATOR—CONTINUED
ALL PUBLIC LIBRARIES

Regional Data

	Min	Q1	Mean	Median	Q3	Max	N
North Atlantic	33,009	52,670	61,297	58,313	68,030	122,001	460
Great Lakes & Plains	25,000	48,130	56,866	55,949	64,257	109,650	557
Southeast	26,542	48,568	59,341	57,265	67,811	106,782	594
West & Southwest	34,476	53,080	65,092	62,535	73,152	140,209	678
ALL REGIONS	25,000	50,482	60,835	58,622	68,661	140,209	2,289

State Data

	Min	Q1	Mean	Median	Q3	Max	N
AK	44,928	44,928	44,928	44,928	44,928	44,928	1
AL	40,601	49,629	60,163	58,081	69,763	84,760	26
AZ	49,643	60,590	69,165	67,059	76,333	110,651	60
CA	41,510	64,288	76,191	72,158	83,878	140,209	161
CO	39,440	49,504	58,184	59,923	65,732	72,530	28
CT	37,214	43,000	63,805	66,675	80,111	89,156	6
FL	39,144	49,550	60,832	57,246	69,994	106,782	249
GA	27,000	53,871	60,251	60,480	68,679	81,876	61
HI	43,824	51,300	64,797	62,424	75,948	100,000	17
IA	53,309	66,559	70,217	70,050	77,160	83,130	9
ID	51,002	51,002	51,002	51,002	51,002	51,002	1
IL	35,100	46,920	56,941	55,000	65,793	87,235	93
IN	37,202	44,803	51,678	49,264	59,935	74,270	107
KS	46,192	50,069	57,495	57,166	62,191	76,190	16
KY	36,250	46,946	53,400	52,434	57,845	67,315	33
LA	31,500	31,750	35,859	33,000	39,968	45,936	4
MA	40,000	48,923	53,407	52,282	58,469	72,512	25
MD	43,687	58,149	71,452	70,813	82,131	122,001	100
ME	33,009	38,755	47,722	46,278	55,361	62,303	7
MI	32,000	48,614	54,738	53,778	62,410	80,208	37

MN	33,883	50,867	60,175	59,025	69,492	83,758	28
MO	43,780	50,188	58,409	58,552	64,501	84,063	55
MS	31,400	42,000	48,191	47,244	53,558	66,389	11
MT	56,222	56,222	56,222	56,222	56,222	56,222	1
NC	26,542	41,112	50,955	48,257	58,338	84,371	19
ND	52,325	52,325	52,325	52,325	52,325	52,325	1
NE	44,247	52,446	57,006	60,189	61,621	68,695	9
NH	43,875	43,875	43,875	43,875	43,875	43,875	1
NJ	38,490	53,450	60,159	57,810	68,060	100,109	99
NM	46,280	50,898	57,123	56,400	62,213	71,843	10
NV	52,270	63,606	76,157	74,402	80,496	123,864	36
NY	36,321	52,926	59,379	57,326	62,924	98,870	203
OH	25,000	49,546	58,675	57,420	65,932	109,650	169
OK	39,132	46,746	55,730	55,860	62,611	85,200	32
OR	34,476	54,012	63,297	63,390	72,156	94,326	22
PA	34,089	42,158	50,158	48,609	58,995	71,470	16
RI	43,243	43,243	47,827	49,652	50,585	50,585	3
SC	40,170	45,572	54,637	52,145	62,536	82,056	47
SD	27,015	27,015	27,015	27,015	27,015	27,015	2
TN	26,936	42,928	52,642	51,209	65,702	73,274	15
TX	34,865	48,277	54,894	52,431	59,760	79,439	195
UT	45,168	52,166	58,505	59,550	65,874	71,496	34
VA	28,000	53,276	64,017	61,674	71,458	105,485	122
WA	45,681	60,624	71,012	67,350	81,037	103,524	79
WI	36,500	50,041	59,333	58,660	65,677	91,200	31
WV	38,017	39,000	41,450	40,500	41,644	49,918	7
WY	40,699	40,699	40,699	40,699	40,699	40,699	1

MANAGER/SUPERVISOR OF SUPPORT STAFF

Persons who supervise support staff in any part of the library but do not supervise professional librarians.
Very Small Public Library (serving a population of less than 10,000)

Regional Data

	Min	Q1	Mean	Median	Q3	Max	N
North Atlantic	30,940	35,304	39,374	39,663	42,668	49,245	9
Great Lakes & Plains	30,722	30,722	31,361	31,361	32,000	32,000	2
Southeast	40,000	40,000	40,000	40,000	40,000	40,000	1
West & Southwest	46,791	46,791	50,071	51,306	52,115	52,115	3
ALL REGIONS	30,722	33,380	40,487	40,000	46,791	52,115	15

State Data

	Min	Q1	Mean	Median	Q3	Max	N
CO	46,791	46,791	50,071	51,306	52,115	52,115	3
FL	40,000	40,000	40,000	40,000	40,000	40,000	1
IA	30,722	30,722	31,361	31,361	32,000	32,000	2
ME	33,380	33,380	39,390	41,959	42,832	42,832	3
NY	30,940	30,940	40,093	40,093	49,245	49,245	2
VT	35,304	36,840	39,003	39,020	41,166	42,668	4

MANAGER/SUPERVISOR OF SUPPORT STAFF—CONTINUED
Small Public Library (serving a population of 10,000 to 25,000)

Regional Data

	Min	Q1	Mean	Median	Q3	Max	N
North Atlantic	22,880	37,260	43,973	44,500	50,000	66,386	15
Great Lakes & Plains	27,000	34,418	39,934	38,455	44,408	60,944	31
Southeast	35,751	35,751	40,465	40,465	45,178	45,178	2
West & Southwest	37,128	44,000	50,996	49,227	54,027	72,685	13
ALL REGIONS	22,880	36,774	43,302	43,500	49,121	72,685	61

State Data

	Min	Q1	Mean	Median	Q3	Max	N
AK	42,506	42,506	46,912	49,004	49,227	49,227	3
AL	35,751	35,751	35,751	35,751	35,751	35,751	1
CA	52,632	52,632	62,659	62,659	72,685	72,685	2
CT	45,500	45,500	47,750	47,750	50,000	50,000	2
IA	43,264	43,264	52,104	52,104	60,944	60,944	2
IL	40,850	40,850	47,118	47,706	52,797	52,797	3
IN	30,394	33,206	36,327	33,506	40,251	44,277	5
KS	27,040	27,040	27,040	27,040	27,040	27,040	1
ME	31,200	31,200	31,200	31,200	31,200	31,200	1
MI	31,249	31,249	35,189	36,774	37,544	37,544	3
MN	46,758	46,758	46,758	46,758	46,758	46,758	1
MO	27,000	27,000	32,000	34,000	35,000	35,000	3
NE	35,235	35,235	35,235	35,235	35,235	35,235	1
NJ	48,425	48,425	55,163	50,677	66,386	66,386	3
NY	34,045	42,567	44,104	44,381	49,121	50,130	6
OH	34,418	37,050	42,971	41,812	49,155	53,580	6
OR	59,830	59,830	61,165	61,165	62,500	62,500	2
PA	22,880	22,880	32,760	32,760	42,640	42,640	2
RI	37,260	37,260	37,260	37,260	37,260	37,260	1
TX	43,500	43,750	46,882	45,000	50,014	54,027	4
VA	45,178	45,178	45,178	45,178	45,178	45,178	1
WI	35,610	36,795	40,387	40,267	44,141	45,245	6
WY	37,128	37,128	43,519	43,519	49,909	49,909	2

MANAGER/SUPERVISOR OF SUPPORT STAFF—CONTINUED
Medium Public Library (serving a population of 25,000 to 99,999)

Regional Data

	Min	Q1	Mean	Median	Q3	Max	N
North Atlantic	37,830	46,314	52,776	50,734	60,628	71,823	36
Great Lakes & Plains	32,240	40,186	49,132	48,419	54,900	81,243	55
Southeast	27,000	37,626	45,479	47,522	52,958	59,528	12
West & Southwest	32,000	41,205	53,341	51,759	61,856	108,696	22
ALL REGIONS	27,000	41,510	50,571	48,939	58,158	108,696	125

	Min	Q1	Mean	Median	Q3	Max	N
CA	35,387	56,160	63,718	61,201	69,264	108,696	10
CO	54,804	54,804	54,804	54,804	54,804	54,804	1
CT	65,221	65,221	68,522	68,522	71,823	71,823	2
FL	50,752	50,752	50,752	50,752	50,752	50,752	1
GA	57,000	57,000	57,000	57,000	57,000	57,000	1
IA	81,243	81,243	81,243	81,243	81,243	81,243	1
IL	35,006	46,956	53,073	51,304	60,147	78,000	23
IN	32,240	32,240	37,697	39,065	41,787	41,787	3
MA	39,930	44,934	47,701	47,022	50,819	56,128	8
MD	47,172	47,172	49,926	50,883	51,724	51,724	3
ME	37,830	41,340	45,855	45,162	52,358	52,583	5
MI	33,280	36,937	50,304	39,860	67,260	74,185	5
MN	40,396	40,396	45,991	45,991	51,586	51,586	2
MO	40,639	40,639	40,946	40,946	41,253	41,253	2
ND	48,771	48,771	51,655	51,016	55,178	55,178	3
NH	46,295	46,295	47,526	47,526	48,757	48,757	2
NJ	41,180	58,158	58,807	61,985	64,627	66,186	10
NV	50,000	50,000	50,000	50,000	50,000	50,000	1
NY	44,000	45,166	55,148	53,279	65,130	70,034	4
OH	32,989	39,889	44,138	44,550	46,996	59,924	12
OR	33,396	33,396	33,396	33,396	33,396	33,396	1
RI	47,937	47,937	49,261	49,261	50,585	50,585	2
TX	32,000	36,820	41,674	42,027	45,089	53,517	8
VA	27,000	40,277	46,005	47,522	52,958	59,528	8
WA	64,740	64,740	64,740	64,740	64,740	64,740	1
WI	40,000	41,246	44,299	43,960	47,353	49,278	4
WV	32,820	32,820	34,975	34,975	37,130	37,130	2

MANAGER/SUPERVISOR OF SUPPORT STAFF—CONTINUED
Large Public Library (serving a population of 100,000 to 499,999)

Regional Data

	Min	Q1	Mean	Median	Q3	Max	N
North Atlantic	35,841	48,605	54,270	52,891	61,691	77,239	34
Great Lakes & Plains	32,947	40,651	49,509	48,872	56,576	88,624	147
Southeast	32,455	40,122	47,979	45,084	53,000	86,783	193
West & Southwest	32,837	45,705	54,779	53,490	62,957	87,875	133
ALL REGIONS	32,455	42,084	50,628	48,852	57,762	88,624	507

State Data

	Min	Q1	Mean	Median	Q3	Max	N
AL	66,394	66,394	66,394	66,394	66,394	66,394	1
AZ	42,526	50,781	57,172	54,616	63,465	75,982	13
CA	44,376	54,828	62,281	61,296	69,761	85,098	28
CO	40,000	41,930	47,413	46,766	50,944	57,421	14
FL	34,923	40,322	45,431	42,437	48,269	84,903	44
IA	48,630	48,630	53,518	51,012	60,911	60,911	3

IL	42,598	50,532	54,770	55,341	57,856	67,256	13
IN	32,947	38,922	46,256	43,298	52,728	65,013	35
KS	49,504	49,504	56,105	56,576	62,234	62,234	3
KY	35,562	37,479	42,777	40,775	46,521	57,174	19
MD	45,269	48,729	53,927	51,855	58,485	67,026	16
MI	33,961	47,590	53,626	53,265	58,175	88,624	24
MN	37,378	46,505	53,800	51,871	62,059	73,256	10
MO	34,418	38,581	44,608	44,179	50,000	57,586	13
MS	35,730	42,000	44,654	44,048	50,600	51,500	6
MT	52,416	52,416	52,416	52,416	52,416	52,416	1
NC	32,455	38,889	51,687	52,136	62,198	78,024	30
NE	36,949	39,248	43,959	44,086	45,959	52,524	10
NJ	36,503	39,939	55,466	58,853	62,695	77,239	11
NV	58,458	61,152	64,044	63,167	65,913	72,416	7
NY	35,841	35,841	37,447	37,447	39,052	39,052	2
OH	37,386	40,467	48,770	44,830	58,552	71,677	32
OK	35,808	35,808	35,808	35,808	35,808	35,808	1
OR	51,180	51,180	51,834	51,834	52,488	52,488	2
PA	48,934	51,815	59,469	52,834	69,613	74,150	5
SC	35,041	39,416	46,471	43,192	52,630	78,097	41
TN	42,397	44,139	52,291	51,109	60,476	66,993	10
TX	32,837	42,269	47,268	46,138	52,135	61,758	24
UT	37,170	38,334	45,437	40,393	47,382	69,956	9
VA	35,035	42,962	50,835	46,522	56,295	86,783	42
WA	42,394	47,964	57,386	55,676	65,146	87,875	34
WI	40,651	45,346	53,221	55,021	61,096	62,192	4

MANAGER/SUPERVISOR OF SUPPORT STAFF—CONTINUED

Very Large Public Library (serving a population of 500,000 or more)

Regional Data

	Min	Q1	Mean	Median	Q3	Max	N
North Atlantic	37,382	49,012	59,690	57,520	67,202	127,197	59
Great Lakes & Plains	32,992	44,639	50,753	48,784	53,967	82,557	48
Southeast	35,432	44,067	53,337	48,425	60,112	121,913	114
West & Southwest	36,768	45,043	54,721	51,418	60,384	116,447	209
ALL REGIONS	32,992	44,850	54,593	51,090	60,674	127,197	430

State Data

	Min	Q1	Mean	Median	Q3	Max	N
AZ	43,610	49,643	58,937	53,633	62,072	109,720	45
CA	41,080	54,766	67,301	65,187	76,482	116,447	23
CO	51,418	53,498	57,640	56,628	61,495	66,456	8
FL	41,241	48,107	61,086	59,592	68,016	121,913	44
GA	35,432	43,000	46,509	45,179	49,344	61,787	37
HI	37,464	45,840	55,412	52,332	60,024	85,008	10
IN	32,992	37,364	42,656	44,297	47,195	51,195	10
KY	38,355	40,872	45,055	45,302	47,724	56,160	19
MD	37,382	47,142	61,839	61,378	72,578	127,197	34

MO	44,782	46,183	49,333	49,708	51,241	56,375	9
NM	43,992	43,992	51,362	53,810	56,285	56,285	3
NV	50,274	54,350	62,576	61,152	68,806	80,496	9
NY	39,716	49,880	56,767	55,883	60,522	85,847	25
OH	41,360	46,293	52,965	51,501	56,388	75,192	28
OK	41,940	48,432	56,481	55,440	65,874	71,760	6
OR	63,855	63,855	63,855	63,855	63,855	63,855	1
TX	36,768	41,440	47,376	45,785	50,419	84,289	97
UT	57,288	57,288	57,288	57,288	57,288	57,288	1
VA	42,269	44,067	58,265	58,336	67,880	75,099	14
WA	66,123	69,368	74,771	73,165	80,576	86,230	6
WI	82,557	82,557	82,557	82,557	82,557	82,557	1

MANAGER/SUPERVISOR OF SUPPORT STAFF—CONTINUED
ALL PUBLIC LIBRARIES

Regional Data

	Min	Q1	Mean	Median	Q3	Max	N
North Atlantic	22,880	45,162	54,123	51,091	61,691	127,197	153
Great Lakes & Plains	27,000	40,251	48,470	47,445	54,325	88,624	283
Southeast	27,000	41,332	49,711	46,664	54,975	121,913	322
West & Southwest	32,000	45,027	54,497	52,152	61,183	116,447	380
ALL REGIONS	22,880	42,640	51,594	49,344	58,458	127,197	1,138

State Data

	Min	Q1	Mean	Median	Q3	Max	N
AK	42,506	42,506	46,912	49,004	49,227	49,227	3
AL	35,751	35,751	51,073	51,073	66,394	66,394	2
AZ	42,526	49,745	58,541	53,935	62,965	109,720	58
CA	35,387	54,766	64,354	61,856	72,800	116,447	63
CO	40,000	46,176	51,150	51,362	56,118	66,456	26
CT	45,500	47,750	58,136	57,611	68,522	71,823	4
FL	34,923	42,401	53,084	48,121	61,783	121,913	90
GA	35,432	43,000	46,785	45,197	49,917	61,787	38
HI	37,464	45,840	55,412	52,332	60,024	85,008	10
IA	30,722	37,632	51,091	49,821	60,928	81,243	8
IL	35,006	47,970	53,181	51,679	58,200	78,000	39
IN	30,394	38,500	44,156	41,787	48,653	65,013	53
KS	27,040	38,272	48,839	53,040	59,405	62,234	4
KY	35,562	38,522	43,916	43,067	47,549	57,174	38
MA	39,930	44,934	47,701	47,022	50,819	56,128	8
MD	37,382	47,983	58,776	55,553	65,990	127,197	53
ME	31,200	37,830	42,072	41,959	45,162	52,583	9
MI	31,249	43,279	51,379	51,428	58,175	88,624	32
MN	37,378	46,505	52,057	50,080	55,432	73,256	13
MO	27,000	38,581	44,511	46,021	50,925	57,586	27
MS	35,730	42,000	44,654	44,048	50,600	51,500	6
MT	52,416	52,416	52,416	52,416	52,416	52,416	1
NC	32,455	38,889	51,687	52,136	62,198	78,024	30

ND	48,771	48,771	51,655	51,016	55,178	55,178	3
NE	35,235	39,006	43,166	43,837	45,959	52,524	11
NH	46,295	46,295	47,526	47,526	48,757	48,757	2
NJ	36,503	49,399	56,820	59,942	64,045	77,239	24
NM	43,992	43,992	51,362	53,810	56,285	56,285	3
NV	50,000	58,458	62,441	62,655	66,144	80,496	17
NY	30,940	44,461	52,807	51,089	60,000	85,847	39
OH	32,989	42,084	49,117	46,366	55,596	75,192	78
OK	35,808	41,940	53,528	52,596	65,874	71,760	7
OR	33,396	51,180	53,875	56,159	62,500	63,855	6
PA	22,880	42,640	51,838	51,815	69,613	74,150	7
RI	37,260	37,260	45,261	47,937	50,585	50,585	3
SC	35,041	39,416	46,471	43,192	52,630	78,097	41
TN	42,397	44,139	52,291	51,109	60,476	66,993	10
TX	32,000	41,458	46,999	45,218	50,721	84,289	133
UT	37,170	38,334	46,622	42,026	54,558	69,956	10
VA	27,000	43,392	51,754	48,614	59,528	86,783	65
VT	35,304	36,840	39,003	39,020	41,166	42,668	4
WA	42,394	49,046	60,110	59,278	67,152	87,875	41
WI	35,610	40,000	47,664	44,141	50,041	82,557	15
WV	32,820	32,820	34,975	34,975	37,130	37,130	2
WY	37,128	37,128	43,519	43,519	49,909	49,909	2

LIBRARIAN WHO DOES NOT SUPERVISE

Full-time staff with master's degrees from programs in library and information studies accredited by the ALA who was not reported earlier and who does not supervise.

Very Small Public Library (serving a population of less than 10,000)

Regional Data

	Min	Q1	Mean	Median	Q3	Max	N
North Atlantic	24,224	37,843	38,098	39,256	40,593	45,406	9
Great Lakes & Plains	25,958	26,000	31,600	29,123	37,490	41,219	7
Southeast	31,475	31,475	35,543	34,146	41,007	41,007	3
West & Southwest	26,363	26,363	26,363	26,363	26,363	26,363	1
ALL REGIONS	24,224	27,952	34,854	36,061	40,417	45,406	20

State Data

	Min	Q1	Mean	Median	Q3	Max	N
AL	31,475	31,475	35,543	34,146	41,007	41,007	3
CT	24,224	24,224	24,224	24,224	24,224	24,224	1
IA	29,123	29,123	29,123	29,123	29,123	29,123	1
IL	37,490	37,490	39,355	39,355	41,219	41,219	2
ME	39,256	39,256	39,925	39,925	40,593	40,593	2
NE	26,000	26,000	26,000	26,000	26,000	26,000	1
NJ	40,240	40,240	40,240	40,240	40,240	40,240	1
NM	26,363	26,363	26,363	26,363	26,363	26,363	1
NY	37,844	37,844	37,844	37,844	37,844	37,844	1
OH	25,958	25,958	29,123	26,780	34,632	34,632	3
RI	34,581	34,581	38,740	38,740	42,898	42,898	2
VT	37,843	37,843	41,625	41,625	45,406	45,406	2

LIBRARIAN WHO DOES NOT SUPERVISE—CONTINUED
Small Public Library (serving a population of 10,000 to 25,000)

Regional Data

	Min	Q1	Mean	Median	Q3	Max	N
North Atlantic	22,880	37,596	46,121	45,122	52,866	76,237	41
Great Lakes & Plains	26,832	35,000	38,716	38,563	41,417	59,328	33
Southeast	32,000	42,349	41,517	43,130	44,075	44,415	6
West & Southwest	35,225	49,930	55,538	54,682	56,556	82,150	6
ALL REGIONS	22,880	36,500	43,616	41,437	49,920	82,150	86

State Data

	Min	Q1	Mean	Median	Q3	Max	N
AL	42,349	42,349	43,256	43,130	44,163	44,415	4
CA	55,464	55,464	64,723	56,556	82,150	82,150	3
IL	30,000	37,098	41,397	39,772	41,993	59,328	16
MA	45,122	45,122	48,087	48,087	51,051	51,051	2
ME	28,600	28,600	33,738	35,054	37,559	37,559	3
MI	42,961	42,961	42,961	42,961	42,961	42,961	1
MO	35,000	35,000	35,000	35,000	35,000	35,000	1
NE	32,532	32,532	32,532	32,532	32,532	32,532	1
NJ	44,730	47,750	55,475	53,546	60,335	76,237	18
NY	36,522	37,523	41,934	40,300	46,148	53,064	9
OH	26,832	32,891	35,334	35,505	39,766	42,217	12
OR	49,930	49,930	51,915	51,915	53,900	53,900	2
PA	22,880	26,520	34,791	37,610	41,653	43,883	8
RI	39,312	39,312	39,312	39,312	39,312	39,312	1
SC	32,000	32,000	32,000	32,000	32,000	32,000	1
VA	44,075	44,075	44,075	44,075	44,075	44,075	1
WI	38,563	38,563	40,395	40,395	42,227	42,227	2
WY	35,225	35,225	35,225	35,225	35,225	35,225	1

LIBRARIAN WHO DOES NOT SUPERVISE—CONTINUED
Medium Public Library (serving a population of 25,000 to 99,999)

Regional Data

	Min	Q1	Mean	Median	Q3	Max	N
North Atlantic	29,065	43,240	49,693	47,699	55,980	83,143	90
Great Lakes & Plains	29,640	38,318	45,552	44,346	50,600	76,000	119
Southeast	22,000	37,336	40,130	39,975	42,582	53,830	36
West & Southwest	27,000	42,411	50,469	47,466	58,800	76,344	51
ALL REGIONS	22,000	40,290	46,999	45,572	52,136	83,143	296

State Data

	Min	Q1	Mean	Median	Q3	Max	N
AL	37,877	39,374	42,494	41,777	44,325	49,837	6
CA	46,275	52,578	59,582	59,290	66,995	76,344	16
CO	45,383	45,383	48,214	47,466	51,792	51,792	3
CT	54,251	54,251	59,333	58,765	64,983	64,983	3

FL	33,634	35,288	38,787	36,775	39,354	53,830	8
IA	45,708	46,030	52,491	51,144	60,065	60,856	6
ID	27,000	27,000	35,049	35,049	43,098	43,098	2
IL	32,390	38,442	47,159	46,569	53,500	76,000	55
IN	34,424	34,882	39,508	38,132	43,423	50,315	12
KY	23,712	23,712	23,712	23,712	23,712	23,712	1
LA	31,796	31,796	34,681	32,994	39,254	39,254	3
MA	38,393	38,500	47,898	51,195	55,558	56,128	7
MD	43,704	43,704	44,273	44,273	44,841	44,841	2
ME	37,412	39,283	42,335	41,067	44,870	49,043	5
MI	35,152	43,340	48,877	49,750	53,560	65,000	15
MN	37,814	37,814	41,360	40,726	45,539	45,539	3
MO	37,406	37,406	38,167	38,348	38,748	38,748	3
ND	40,427	40,427	41,384	41,384	42,341	42,341	2
NH	35,353	35,353	36,748	36,748	38,142	38,142	2
NJ	41,000	45,802	51,788	50,678	56,377	71,710	34
NV	45,000	45,000	45,000	45,000	45,000	45,000	1
NY	41,545	44,321	54,048	50,237	59,076	83,143	25
OH	29,640	36,379	41,996	41,808	45,923	54,054	19
OR	39,804	39,804	41,790	41,790	43,776	43,776	2
PA	29,065	29,502	35,383	31,886	41,943	47,333	8
RI	45,614	45,883	47,572	47,045	49,261	50,585	4
TX	39,543	41,775	46,348	46,197	48,033	65,000	19
UT	41,700	41,740	41,882	41,760	41,911	42,299	5
VA	39,010	39,854	42,921	41,793	43,051	51,768	17
WA	59,748	59,748	62,420	62,772	64,740	64,740	3
WI	32,000	40,708	46,379	49,493	52,051	54,531	4
WV	22,000	22,000	22,000	22,000	22,000	22,000	1

LIBRARIAN WHO DOES NOT SUPERVISE—CONTINUED
Large Public Library (serving a population of 100,000 to 499,999)

Regional Data

	Min	Q1	Mean	Median	Q3	Max	N
North Atlantic	33,374	42,883	50,621	50,500	56,993	77,172	97
Great Lakes & Plains	23,478	41,251	46,355	46,197	50,645	71,496	323
Southeast	30,000	38,417	43,862	42,104	48,027	73,943	241
West & Southwest	29,247	43,680	51,087	50,097	58,053	83,172	218
ALL REGIONS	23,478	40,657	47,316	46,280	52,363	83,172	879

State Data

	Min	Q1	Mean	Median	Q3	Max	N
AZ	42,342	50,325	58,600	59,114	65,354	75,983	19
CA	41,683	49,717	57,111	56,010	62,556	83,172	54
CO	35,734	45,937	49,406	50,939	52,689	59,891	31
FL	36,057	39,922	44,709	44,449	48,027	69,194	75
GA	48,225	48,225	56,184	55,869	64,459	64,459	3
IA	45,635	45,635	49,565	49,565	53,494	53,494	2
IL	34,406	43,156	49,810	49,192	53,768	70,239	31

IN	30,451	38,972	44,197	43,719	48,980	65,998	56
KS	38,788	46,093	47,315	47,216	49,313	54,101	37
KY	32,240	34,976	38,829	37,596	41,392	52,709	18
LA	30,000	30,000	30,777	30,777	31,553	31,553	2
MA	55,385	55,385	55,385	55,385	55,385	55,385	1
MD	33,374	41,450	46,099	43,005	50,721	65,151	26
MI	23,478	43,472	47,863	48,578	51,875	65,263	34
MN	25,521	44,672	49,627	49,242	52,313	66,734	22
MO	35,693	41,766	46,595	45,406	50,077	71,496	33
MS	35,887	35,887	40,214	39,868	44,887	44,887	3
MT	43,680	43,680	43,680	43,680	43,680	43,680	2
NC	32,455	38,596	44,270	44,000	50,000	59,171	26
NE	35,303	35,303	45,278	45,377	55,153	55,153	3
NJ	34,500	46,844	52,557	52,707	58,636	77,172	64
NV	52,447	52,447	52,447	52,447	52,447	52,447	1
NY	40,943	40,943	50,970	55,883	56,083	56,083	3
OH	32,940	38,064	42,400	42,292	46,312	52,980	84
OK	35,808	36,888	39,773	39,132	40,308	46,728	5
OR	32,198	32,198	44,125	46,428	53,748	53,748	3
PA	42,806	42,806	46,585	45,117	51,833	51,833	3
SC	32,400	36,328	39,883	39,138	41,710	52,630	62
TN	36,400	38,984	45,605	43,024	49,367	73,274	14
TX	29,247	40,024	42,108	41,707	45,242	63,502	47
UT	37,419	38,463	49,498	48,370	59,758	65,021	10
VA	37,540	42,989	50,152	49,446	55,586	73,943	38
WA	38,408	45,861	53,544	52,426	59,278	83,040	46
WI	40,651	51,272	54,736	55,806	58,916	66,170	21

LIBRARIAN WHO DOES NOT SUPERVISE—CONTINUED

Very Large Public Library (serving a population of 500,000 or more)

Regional Data

	Min	Q1	Mean	Median	Q3	Max	N
North Atlantic	37,630	43,904	50,097	47,164	51,647	88,310	178
Great Lakes & Plains	27,899	40,706	47,446	45,347	52,478	75,192	135
Southeast	22,089	42,030	50,557	47,246	57,059	96,855	287
West & Southwest	32,160	43,404	50,306	47,673	56,534	92,317	383
ALL REGIONS	22,089	42,759	49,949	47,162	54,805	96,855	983

State Data

	Min	Q1	Mean	Median	Q3	Max	N
AZ	41,704	46,353	53,481	51,033	61,890	78,561	32
CA	40,308	50,064	57,950	56,722	64,792	80,288	49
CO	38,563	42,598	46,897	43,867	49,920	60,320	14
FL	22,089	42,151	50,988	47,532	57,649	96,855	235
GA	34,091	40,632	46,835	44,784	50,328	71,460	30
HI	40,512	45,588	51,170	51,300	56,040	62,424	13
IN	27,899	37,766	40,837	40,542	44,832	55,373	58
KY	39,084	39,877	43,820	41,711	43,786	54,642	5

MD	37,630	44,076	57,355	53,251	68,890	88,310	49
MO	41,135	42,697	49,396	48,753	54,805	65,569	19
NM	38,085	39,011	42,744	40,945	46,478	51,002	4
NV	44,699	46,456	51,811	50,274	56,534	63,606	15
NY	38,800	43,904	47,341	47,121	48,871	79,243	129
OH	38,896	46,207	54,434	53,529	61,277	75,192	48
OK	34,668	39,216	44,922	42,848	46,925	77,400	39
OR	47,899	51,636	55,663	54,758	58,109	68,403	8
TX	32,160	39,865	44,553	44,330	47,051	64,792	134
UT	36,312	43,944	49,036	48,288	54,456	61,728	28
VA	42,026	45,119	53,145	50,867	60,078	68,395	17
WA	43,763	53,432	61,828	61,392	66,123	92,317	47
WI	42,594	45,347	48,528	49,092	50,896	53,832	10

LIBRARIAN WHO DOES NOT SUPERVISE—CONTINUED
ALL PUBLIC LIBRARIES

Regional Data

	Min	Q1	Mean	Median	Q3	Max	N
North Atlantic	22,880	42,883	49,479	47,278	54,102	88,310	415
Great Lakes & Plains	23,478	40,070	45,863	45,159	50,606	76,000	617
Southeast	22,000	39,653	46,913	44,928	51,734	96,855	573
West & Southwest	26,363	43,368	50,588	48,557	56,748	92,317	659
ALL REGIONS	22,000	41,278	48,167	46,426	53,239	96,855	2,264

State Data

	Min	Q1	Mean	Median	Q3	Max	N
AL	31,475	39,374	41,124	42,349	43,911	49,837	13
AZ	41,704	47,694	55,388	53,226	62,690	78,561	51
CA	40,308	50,752	57,959	56,646	64,116	83,172	122
CO	35,734	44,091	48,599	48,910	52,515	60,320	48
CT	24,224	39,238	50,556	56,508	61,874	64,983	4
FL	22,089	41,142	49,200	46,623	53,830	96,855	318
GA	34,091	41,436	47,685	45,368	50,832	71,460	33
HI	40,512	45,588	51,170	51,300	56,040	62,424	13
IA	29,123	45,708	49,244	48,089	54,199	60,856	9
ID	27,000	27,000	35,049	35,049	43,098	43,098	2
IL	30,000	40,004	46,913	46,080	52,136	76,000	104
IN	27,899	37,747	42,203	41,624	45,409	65,998	126
KS	38,788	46,093	47,315	47,216	49,313	54,101	37
KY	23,712	35,179	39,239	38,360	41,999	54,642	24
LA	30,000	31,553	33,119	31,796	32,994	39,254	5
MA	38,393	43,603	48,684	51,123	55,385	56,128	10
MD	33,374	42,174	53,214	50,038	61,680	88,310	77
ME	28,600	37,412	39,274	39,270	41,067	49,043	10
MI	23,478	43,410	48,069	48,849	52,042	65,263	50
MN	25,521	44,250	48,635	49,020	51,236	66,734	25
MO	35,000	41,870	46,887	45,389	50,194	71,496	56
MS	35,887	35,887	40,214	39,868	44,887	44,887	3

MT	43,680	43,680	43,680	43,680	43,680	43,680	2
NC	32,455	38,596	44,270	44,000	50,000	59,171	26
ND	40,427	40,427	41,384	41,384	42,341	42,341	2
NE	26,000	32,532	38,873	35,303	45,377	55,153	5
NH	35,353	35,353	36,748	36,748	38,142	38,142	2
NJ	34,500	46,774	52,677	52,000	58,158	77,172	117
NM	26,363	38,085	39,468	39,936	41,954	51,002	5
NV	44,699	46,456	51,448	50,274	56,534	63,606	17
NY	36,522	43,897	48,062	47,121	49,752	83,143	167
OH	25,958	38,418	45,083	43,387	49,920	75,192	166
OK	34,668	39,149	44,337	41,850	46,608	77,400	44
OR	32,198	46,428	51,006	52,409	55,562	68,403	15
PA	22,880	29,429	36,902	39,000	43,883	51,833	19
RI	34,581	39,312	43,868	45,614	47,937	50,585	7
SC	32,000	36,263	39,757	39,136	41,710	52,630	63
TN	36,400	38,984	45,605	43,024	49,367	73,274	14
TX	29,247	40,142	44,149	44,036	46,865	65,000	200
UT	36,312	41,760	48,312	46,992	54,648	65,021	43
VA	37,540	41,838	49,082	46,823	55,165	73,943	73
VT	37,843	37,843	41,625	41,625	45,406	45,406	2
WA	38,408	50,269	57,877	57,060	64,629	92,317	96
WI	32,000	47,938	51,380	51,272	55,806	66,170	37
WV	22,000	22,000	22,000	22,000	22,000	22,000	1
WY	35,225	35,225	35,225	35,225	35,225	35,225	1

BEGINNING LIBRARIAN

Full-time staff hired in the last six months with master's degrees from programs in library and information studies accredited by the ALA, but with no professional experience after receiving the degree.
Very Small Public Library (serving a population of less than 10,000)

Regional Data

	Min	Q1	Mean	Median	Q3	Max	N
North Atlantic	22,650	36,197	47,013	46,050	54,250	84,341	12
Great Lakes & Plains	23,858	26,000	30,227	29,568	33,280	39,089	6
Southeast	40,000	40,000	40,000	40,000	40,000	40,000	1
West & Southwest	35,000	35,000	46,542	46,542	58,084	58,084	2
ALL REGIONS	22,650	33,280	41,838	39,089	46,540	84,341	21

State Data

	Min	Q1	Mean	Median	Q3	Max	N
AZ	58,084	58,084	58,084	58,084	58,084	58,084	1
CT	46,540	46,540	46,540	46,540	46,540	46,540	1
FL	40,000	40,000	40,000	40,000	40,000	40,000	1
IN	28,975	28,975	29,568	29,568	30,160	30,160	2
KS	23,858	23,858	29,649	26,000	39,089	39,089	3
MA	58,000	58,000	58,000	58,000	58,000	58,000	1
ME	34,536	34,536	34,536	34,536	34,536	34,536	1
NH	34,549	34,549	34,549	34,549	34,549	34,549	1
NY	22,650	37,844	49,219	46,100	54,250	84,341	7

OH	33,280	33,280	33,280	33,280	33,280	33,280	1
OR	35,000	35,000	35,000	35,000	35,000	35,000	1
RI	46,000	46,000	46,000	46,000	46,000	46,000	1

BEGINNING LIBRARIAN—CONTINUED
Small Public Library (serving a population of 10,000 to 25,000)

Regional Data

	Min	Q1	Mean	Median	Q3	Max	N
North Atlantic	28,000	38,250	43,266	42,642	46,717	63,000	12
Great Lakes & Plains	28,000	32,246	40,565	36,745	45,918	56,971	20
Southeast	34,000	34,000	65,554	65,554	97,107	97,107	2
West & Southwest	39,641	39,641	39,641	39,641	39,641	39,641	1
ALL REGIONS	28,000	34,000	42,892	40,000	45,934	97,107	35

State Data

	Min	Q1	Mean	Median	Q3	Max	N
AL	97,107	97,107	97,107	97,107	97,107	97,107	1
IL	31,200	33,000	36,182	35,100	38,821	44,100	7
IN	28,000	28,000	28,000	28,000	28,000	28,000	1
KY	34,000	34,000	34,000	34,000	34,000	34,000	1
MA	57,000	57,000	60,000	60,000	63,000	63,000	2
MI	28,600	28,600	29,925	29,925	31,249	31,249	2
MN	56,971	56,971	56,971	56,971	56,971	56,971	4
NJ	28,000	40,000	40,942	43,277	45,934	47,500	5
NY	42,006	42,006	43,253	43,253	44,500	44,500	2
OH	31,493	31,493	33,551	33,551	35,610	35,610	2
PA	29,870	29,870	35,990	36,500	41,600	41,600	3
TX	39,641	39,641	39,641	39,641	39,641	39,641	1
WI	37,440	41,679	43,799	45,918	45,918	45,918	4

BEGINNING LIBRARIAN—CONTINUED
Medium Public Library (serving a population of 25,000 to 99,999)

Regional Data

	Min	Q1	Mean	Median	Q3	Max	N
North Atlantic	35,631	39,000	45,188	42,000	44,189	90,000	11
Great Lakes & Plains	24,988	34,500	42,276	37,590	47,040	85,290	24
Southeast	31,200	36,302	41,192	43,995	44,778	46,562	9
West & Southwest	32,552	35,472	44,266	44,652	51,624	53,880	9
ALL REGIONS	24,988	35,588	43,034	40,000	45,000	90,000	53

State Data

	Min	Q1	Mean	Median	Q3	Max	N
AL	35,006	35,006	35,006	35,006	35,006	35,006	1
CA	32,552	32,552	43,216	43,216	53,880	53,880	2
CO	35,472	35,472	35,472	35,472	35,472	35,472	1
FL	43,614	43,614	43,614	43,614	43,614	43,614	1
GA	45,000	45,000	45,000	45,000	45,000	45,000	1

IA	38,334	38,334	38,334	38,334	38,334	38,334	1
IL	34,000	34,500	44,547	36,194	56,387	68,211	8
IN	24,988	33,758	37,430	38,180	38,230	51,996	5
MA	90,000	90,000	90,000	90,000	90,000	90,000	1
ME	35,631	35,631	35,631	35,631	35,631	35,631	2
MI	50,179	50,179	50,179	50,179	50,179	50,179	1
MN	35,609	35,609	35,609	35,609	35,609	35,609	1
NC	43,995	44,134	44,902	44,526	45,670	46,562	4
ND	85,290	85,290	85,290	85,290	85,290	85,290	1
NJ	39,000	39,650	42,258	43,277	44,189	44,359	7
NV	53,000	53,000	53,000	53,000	53,000	53,000	1
NY	40,000	40,000	40,000	40,000	40,000	40,000	1
OH	33,014	33,014	36,200	35,588	39,998	39,998	3
OR	44,652	44,652	49,300	51,624	51,624	51,624	3
TX	34,092	34,092	37,794	37,794	41,496	41,496	2
VA	36,302	36,302	36,302	36,302	36,302	36,302	1
WI	30,160	33,080	38,271	38,809	43,462	45,305	4
WV	31,200	31,200	31,200	31,200	31,200	31,200	1

BEGINNING LIBRARIAN—CONTINUED

Large Public Library (serving a population of 100,000 to 499,999)

Regional Data

	Min	Q1	Mean	Median	Q3	Max	N
North Atlantic	35,000	40,170	43,046	43,527	46,332	50,735	14
Great Lakes & Plains	28,683	32,940	38,439	38,263	43,482	51,414	27
Southeast	27,596	35,652	39,059	38,066	41,995	54,233	50
West & Southwest	28,533	38,407	45,332	43,264	51,522	75,000	38
ALL REGIONS	27,596	35,991	41,210	40,014	45,788	75,000	129

State Data

	Min	Q1	Mean	Median	Q3	Max	N
AL	38,896	38,896	38,896	38,896	38,896	38,896	1
AZ	37,059	43,199	46,657	49,670	50,114	50,228	4
CA	36,108	44,319	51,211	51,522	55,848	75,000	19
CO	36,707	36,707	37,739	37,739	38,771	38,771	2
FL	32,947	36,989	41,886	41,359	45,822	54,233	24
IA	44,649	44,649	44,649	44,649	44,649	44,649	1
IL	35,360	35,360	37,687	37,687	40,014	40,014	2
IN	28,683	28,902	30,618	29,120	32,334	35,547	4
KY	33,365	33,365	33,365	33,365	33,365	33,365	1
LA	35,991	35,991	35,991	35,991	35,991	35,991	1
MA	43,054	43,054	44,643	44,643	46,232	46,232	3
MD	40,170	40,170	40,834	40,834	41,497	41,497	2
MI	38,263	40,206	42,705	42,250	46,300	46,961	6
MN	39,333	39,333	39,333	39,333	39,333	39,333	1
MO	34,500	34,500	34,500	34,500	34,500	34,500	1
MS	31,065	31,065	31,533	31,533	32,000	32,000	2
MT	32,614	32,614	32,614	32,614	32,614	32,614	1

NC	32,455	34,370	35,918	35,229	36,768	40,769	5
NE	42,408	43,938	47,551	48,191	51,165	51,414	4
NJ	35,000	36,503	40,849	42,000	44,000	46,740	5
NY	38,313	42,323	45,703	46,881	49,083	50,735	4
OH	31,242	32,304	33,311	32,940	34,900	35,900	7
OK	35,808	35,808	35,808	35,808	35,808	35,808	1
OR	42,120	42,120	44,660	44,660	47,200	47,200	2
SC	32,400	35,131	35,534	35,652	36,329	38,160	5
TN	27,596	27,596	33,290	33,290	38,984	38,984	2
TX	28,533	29,809	34,695	34,792	39,582	40,664	4
UT	37,170	37,170	37,170	37,170	37,170	37,170	1
VA	35,840	36,920	39,170	38,484	41,570	44,291	9
WA	38,407	38,407	38,454	38,454	38,500	38,500	4
WI	41,908	41,908	41,908	41,908	41,908	41,908	1

BEGINNING LIBRARIAN—CONTINUED

Very Large Public Library (serving a population of 500,000 or more)

Regional Data

	Min	Q1	Mean	Median	Q3	Max	N
North Atlantic	34,127	35,801	37,672	38,410	39,295	39,295	7
Great Lakes & Plains	37,640	38,896	41,855	41,126	43,875	50,057	7
Southeast	34,091	36,492	40,437	40,840	42,887	52,571	10
West & Southwest	32,544	40,093	45,008	42,973	47,673	69,389	93
ALL REGIONS	32,544	39,553	43,990	41,489	46,350	69,389	117

State Data

	Min	Q1	Mean	Median	Q3	Max	N
AZ	40,331	40,331	40,716	40,716	41,101	41,101	2
CA	40,308	41,687	48,939	44,695	54,674	69,389	16
CO	37,003	37,003	37,003	37,003	37,003	37,003	1
FL	35,000	35,000	37,882	37,176	41,471	41,471	3
GA	34,091	35,292	40,949	38,568	46,607	52,571	4
HI	40,512	40,512	40,512	40,512	40,512	40,512	1
MD	34,127	34,964	36,455	36,642	37,946	38,410	4
NV	42,973	42,973	42,973	42,973	42,973	42,973	3
NY	39,295	39,295	39,295	39,295	39,295	39,295	3
OH	38,896	38,896	43,438	41,360	50,057	50,057	3
OK	35,817	35,817	36,181	36,181	36,545	36,545	2
TX	32,544	39,894	44,501	42,319	46,835	63,907	62
UT	36,312	36,312	36,312	36,312	36,312	36,312	1
VA	41,037	41,037	42,308	42,887	43,000	43,000	3
WA	42,494	43,763	49,420	47,673	54,516	58,654	5
WI	37,640	38,835	40,668	40,578	42,501	43,875	4

Regional Data

	Min	Q1	Mean	Median	Q3	Max	N
North Atlantic	22,650	38,079	43,692	42,003	46,166	90,000	56
Great Lakes & Plains	23,858	33,278	39,739	37,910	44,375	85,290	84
Southeast	27,596	35,746	40,266	38,690	43,125	97,107	72
West & Southwest	28,533	39,585	45,031	42,973	50,228	75,000	143
ALL REGIONS	22,650	36,302	42,601	41,018	46,214	97,107	355

State Data

	Min	Q1	Mean	Median	Q3	Max	N
AL	35,006	35,006	57,003	38,896	97,107	97,107	3
AZ	37,059	40,331	46,592	49,339	50,228	58,084	7
CA	32,552	42,372	49,796	48,080	54,841	75,000	37
CO	35,472	36,090	36,988	36,855	37,887	38,771	4
CT	46,540	46,540	46,540	46,540	46,540	46,540	1
FL	32,947	37,176	41,466	41,184	44,294	54,233	29
GA	34,091	36,492	41,759	40,643	45,000	52,571	5
HI	40,512	40,512	40,512	40,512	40,512	40,512	1
IA	38,334	38,334	41,492	41,492	44,649	44,649	2
IL	31,200	34,500	40,295	35,388	40,014	68,211	17
IN	24,988	28,829	33,063	29,640	36,864	51,996	12
KS	23,858	23,858	29,649	26,000	39,089	39,089	3
KY	33,365	33,365	33,683	33,683	34,000	34,000	2
LA	35,991	35,991	35,991	35,991	35,991	35,991	1
MA	43,054	44,643	57,418	57,000	63,000	90,000	7
MD	34,127	35,801	37,915	37,946	40,170	41,497	6
ME	34,536	34,536	35,266	35,631	35,631	35,631	3
MI	28,600	38,263	40,695	41,018	46,300	50,179	9
MN	35,609	39,333	50,471	56,971	56,971	56,971	6
MO	34,500	34,500	34,500	34,500	34,500	34,500	1
MS	31,065	31,065	31,533	31,533	32,000	32,000	2
MT	32,614	32,614	32,614	32,614	32,614	32,614	1
NC	32,455	35,229	39,911	40,769	44,273	46,562	9
ND	85,290	85,290	85,290	85,290	85,290	85,290	1
NE	42,408	43,938	47,551	48,191	51,165	51,414	4
NH	34,549	34,549	34,549	34,549	34,549	34,549	1
NJ	28,000	39,650	41,456	43,277	44,189	47,500	17
NV	42,973	42,973	45,480	42,973	47,986	53,000	4
NY	22,650	39,295	45,396	44,500	47,430	84,341	17
OH	31,242	32,777	35,779	34,090	37,398	50,057	16
OK	35,808	35,808	36,057	35,817	36,545	36,545	3
OR	35,000	42,120	45,370	45,926	51,624	51,624	6
PA	29,870	29,870	35,990	36,500	41,600	41,600	3
RI	46,000	46,000	46,000	46,000	46,000	46,000	1
SC	32,400	35,131	35,534	35,652	36,329	38,160	5
TN	27,596	27,596	33,290	33,290	38,984	38,984	2

TX	28,533	39,585	43,668	41,489	46,350	63,907	69
UT	36,312	36,312	36,741	36,741	37,170	37,170	2
VA	35,840	36,920	39,674	39,560	42,600	44,291	13
WA	38,407	38,500	44,546	42,494	47,673	58,654	9
WI	30,160	37,640	40,989	41,618	45,305	45,918	13
WV	31,200	31,200	31,200	31,200	31,200	31,200	1

Academic (Two-Year College to University; Regional, State)

DIRECTOR/DEAN/CHIEF OFFICER
Chief officer of the library or library system.
Two-Year College

Regional Data

	Min	Q1	Mean	Median	Q3	Max	N
North Atlantic	38,433	68,646	75,674	84,235	88,910	93,901	13
Great Lakes & Plains	34,000	55,956	72,857	68,061	95,500	102,000	12
Southeast	37,440	55,488	63,299	63,496	70,000	104,900	18
West & Southwest	39,150	62,216	76,116	70,400	84,500	162,700	46
ALL REGIONS	34,000	60,000	73,020	68,646	84,500	162,700	89

State Data

	Min	Q1	Mean	Median	Q3	Max	N
AK	62,216	62,216	62,216	62,216	62,216	62,216	1
AZ	79,883	79,883	83,836	83,836	87,788	87,788	2
CA	86,928	88,000	111,146	112,390	120,381	162,700	9
CO	50,000	50,000	57,667	55,000	68,000	68,000	3
CT	93,901	93,901	93,901	93,901	93,901	93,901	2
FL	37,440	45,136	65,605	60,040	86,074	104,900	4
GA	55,488	60,000	62,096	60,000	64,992	70,000	5
HI	63,419	63,419	73,099	73,099	82,779	82,779	2
IA	66,000	66,000	67,462	67,462	68,923	68,923	2
IL	95,000	95,000	98,500	98,500	102,000	102,000	2
KS	34,000	34,000	56,174	54,521	80,000	80,000	3
LA	70,415	70,415	70,415	70,415	70,415	70,415	1
MA	75,000	75,000	81,746	81,746	88,492	88,492	2
MD	68,646	68,646	68,646	68,646	68,646	68,646	1
MI	67,199	67,199	82,962	82,962	98,724	98,724	2
MO	56,891	56,891	56,891	56,891	56,891	56,891	1
NC	39,500	50,750	58,321	63,724	65,892	66,335	4
ND	55,020	55,020	55,020	55,020	55,020	55,020	1
NJ	88,910	88,910	89,240	88,910	89,900	89,900	3
NM	45,736	45,736	45,736	45,736	45,736	45,736	1
NV	63,492	63,492	73,996	73,996	84,500	84,500	2
NY	38,433	38,433	64,889	72,000	84,235	84,235	3
OH	96,000	96,000	96,000	96,000	96,000	96,000	1
OK	67,200	67,200	67,200	67,200	67,200	67,200	1
PA	45,438	45,438	50,719	50,719	56,000	56,000	2
SC	55,056	55,056	67,094	71,225	75,000	75,000	3
TN	61,500	61,500	61,500	61,500	61,500	61,500	1
TX	39,150	60,250	65,705	64,252	71,147	95,034	16
UT	54,000	54,000	54,000	54,000	54,000	54,000	1
WA	60,000	64,000	73,156	74,173	79,980	84,000	7
WY	73,613	73,613	73,613	73,613	73,613	73,613	1

DIRECTOR/DEAN/CHIEF OFFICER—CONTINUED
Four-Year College

Regional Data

	Min	Q1	Mean	Median	Q3	Max	N
North Atlantic	42,000	63,500	93,618	89,010	115,905	163,000	29
Great Lakes & Plains	41,000	54,527	66,380	61,998	75,588	125,000	32
Southeast	40,000	55,248	68,042	69,672	75,000	103,000	25
West & Southwest	36,071	51,750	66,959	65,948	83,600	95,778	16
ALL REGIONS	36,071	55,908	74,622	69,318	84,872	163,000	102

State Data

	Min	Q1	Mean	Median	Q3	Max	N
AL	49,141	49,141	50,428	50,428	51,715	51,715	2
AR	74,271	74,271	74,271	74,271	74,271	74,271	1
CA	77,976	77,976	78,988	78,988	80,000	80,000	2
CO	58,000	58,000	58,000	58,000	58,000	58,000	1
DE	50,000	50,000	50,000	50,000	50,000	50,000	1
FL	59,317	59,317	65,239	65,200	71,200	71,200	3
GA	62,276	62,276	70,859	62,500	87,800	87,800	3
IA	50,000	63,996	71,311	70,000	80,000	92,560	5
ID	71,500	71,500	71,500	71,500	71,500	71,500	1
IL	50,000	50,000	58,801	60,000	66,404	66,404	3
IN	56,000	56,000	63,758	56,100	79,175	79,175	3
KY	84,390	84,390	84,390	84,390	84,390	84,390	1
LA	51,681	51,681	51,681	51,681	51,681	51,681	1
MA	64,158	98,100	118,747	115,905	152,570	163,000	5
ME	60,492	64,500	76,036	66,681	79,508	109,000	5
MI	45,720	45,720	53,573	55,000	60,000	60,000	3
MN	55,189	62,568	78,784	70,974	95,000	118,000	4
MO	47,500	47,500	47,500	47,500	47,500	47,500	1
MS	75,000	75,000	75,000	75,000	75,000	75,000	1
MT	42,000	42,000	42,000	42,000	42,000	42,000	1
NC	51,000	60,500	81,299	85,597	102,097	103,000	4
ND	57,000	57,000	57,000	57,000	57,000	57,000	1
NE	54,053	54,053	59,808	59,808	65,563	65,563	2
NJ	61,000	61,000	97,342	106,026	125,000	125,000	3
NY	42,000	42,000	87,424	84,106	136,167	136,167	3
OH	41,000	45,000	66,882	55,908	84,872	125,000	7
OK	36,071	36,071	47,824	51,000	56,400	56,400	3
OR	90,300	90,300	90,300	90,300	90,300	90,300	1
PA	53,500	63,500	97,836	97,285	135,603	151,861	11
SC	74,961	74,961	79,300	78,441	84,497	84,497	3
SD	68,963	68,963	75,884	75,884	82,804	82,804	2
TN	40,000	40,000	51,891	46,000	69,672	69,672	3
TX	50,000	51,250	71,370	69,850	91,489	95,778	4
UT	71,602	71,602	71,602	71,602	71,602	71,602	1
VA	61,538	61,538	66,269	66,269	71,000	71,000	2
VT	60,500	60,500	60,500	60,500	60,500	60,500	1

2008 ALA-APA Librarian Salary Survey

Academic (Two-Year College to University; Regional, State)

WA	60,395	60,395	75,505	75,505	90,614	90,614	2
WI	80,000	80,000	80,000	80,000	80,000	80,000	1
WV	55,248	55,248	55,248	55,248	55,248	55,248	1

DIRECTOR/DEAN/CHIEF OFFICER—CONTINUED
University (includes ARL data)

Regional Data

	Min	Q1	Mean	Median	Q3	Max	N
North Atlantic	48,000	85,800	120,643	106,000	151,841	281,400	44
Great Lakes & Plains	46,000	66,718	107,654	96,469	123,333	331,200	57
Southeast	40,800	86,135	109,250	105,840	127,251	240,000	55
West & Southwest	54,014	86,683	124,357	123,688	154,801	204,500	42
ALL REGIONS	40,800	81,000	114,527	105,726	137,357	331,200	198

State Data

	Min	Q1	Mean	Median	Q3	Max	N
AL	101,000	101,000	143,129	162,150	166,238	166,238	3
AR	51,989	57,912	73,125	68,255	88,338	104,000	4
AZ	114,920	114,920	134,861	134,861	154,801	154,801	2
CA	59,000	136,080	152,130	156,000	176,500	204,500	13
CO	140,472	140,472	152,288	142,643	173,748	173,748	3
CT	86,599	86,599	106,330	116,196	116,196	116,196	3
DC	92,372	102,386	146,093	141,700	189,800	208,600	4
FL	86,135	105,840	125,068	121,813	135,827	170,000	10
GA	71,960	90,000	93,963	96,288	99,308	109,936	6
HI	66,600	66,600	108,300	108,300	150,000	150,000	2
IA	66,000	66,000	121,724	121,724	177,448	177,448	2
ID	125,424	125,424	125,424	125,424	125,424	125,424	1
IL	46,000	65,300	130,233	113,432	212,000	239,500	7
IN	80,829	87,630	104,091	96,350	125,272	130,376	5
KS	51,000	51,000	121,600	145,000	168,800	168,800	3
KY	66,836	108,675	105,068	114,120	115,000	120,709	5
LA	49,979	67,828	86,861	85,000	93,487	138,010	5
MA	76,146	79,400	129,284	85,000	159,872	246,000	5
MD	62,395	99,500	103,679	108,000	120,850	127,650	5
ME	95,215	95,215	95,215	95,215	95,215	95,215	1
MI	64,000	90,399	142,897	103,392	165,000	331,200	6
MN	65,576	94,622	97,922	99,000	106,000	123,333	6
MO	61,673	67,813	106,328	94,077	121,727	220,000	9
MS	78,500	78,500	78,500	78,500	78,500	78,500	1
MT	55,000	55,000	91,400	100,000	119,200	119,200	3
NC	40,800	76,868	108,568	101,741	123,969	222,585	8
ND	52,955	57,845	73,461	62,882	86,753	119,775	8
NE	62,400	62,400	62,400	62,400	62,400	62,400	1
NH	211,725	211,725	211,725	211,725	211,725	211,725	1
NJ	111,240	116,862	127,861	124,586	138,859	151,031	4
NM	72,000	72,000	72,000	72,000	72,000	72,000	1
NV	198,523	198,523	198,523	198,523	198,523	198,523	1

NY	68,662	90,850	118,604	104,000	153,340	169,416	7
OH	62,987	91,122	115,974	119,629	140,825	161,650	4
OK	70,944	70,944	112,688	112,688	154,431	154,431	2
OR	54,014	54,014	81,338	90,000	100,000	100,000	3
PA	62,280	75,748	126,954	90,000	200,253	281,400	11
RI	58,000	58,000	73,500	73,500	89,000	89,000	2
SC	150,000	150,000	150,000	150,000	150,000	150,000	1
TN	90,000	90,000	90,000	90,000	90,000	90,000	1
TX	74,220	78,500	107,158	90,000	121,951	197,062	7
UT	109,000	109,000	109,000	109,000	109,000	109,000	1
VA	59,245	108,000	127,138	116,399	131,826	240,000	10
VT	48,000	48,000	48,000	48,000	48,000	48,000	1
WA	73,997	73,997	78,594	78,594	83,191	83,191	2
WI	82,459	84,602	96,685	91,771	99,454	130,053	6
WV	54,363	54,363	54,363	54,363	54,363	54,363	1

DIRECTOR/DEAN/CHIEF OFFICER—CONTINUED
ALL ACADEMIC LIBRARIES

Regional Data

	Min	Q1	Mean	Median	Q3	Max	N
North Atlantic	38,433	72,000	104,732	91,840	122,484	281,400	86
Great Lakes & Plains	34,000	60,000	90,443	80,000	105,612	331,200	101
Southeast	37,440	62,276	90,298	81,445	109,936	240,000	98
West & Southwest	36,071	63,746	94,189	80,078	119,162	204,500	104
ALL REGIONS	34,000	63,996	94,567	84,500	114,000	331,200	389

State Data

	Min	Q1	Mean	Median	Q3	Max	N
AK	62,216	62,216	62,216	62,216	62,216	62,216	1
AL	49,141	51,715	106,049	101,000	162,150	166,238	5
AR	51,989	63,834	73,354	72,676	74,271	104,000	5
AZ	79,883	83,836	109,348	101,354	134,861	154,801	4
CA	59,000	95,594	130,666	127,000	162,850	204,500	24
CO	50,000	55,000	98,266	68,000	142,643	173,748	7
CT	86,599	93,901	101,359	93,901	116,196	116,196	5
DC	92,372	102,386	146,093	141,700	189,800	208,600	4
DE	50,000	50,000	50,000	50,000	50,000	50,000	1
FL	37,440	67,248	100,518	104,900	124,450	170,000	17
GA	55,488	62,276	77,631	70,980	96,075	109,936	14
HI	63,419	65,010	90,700	74,690	116,390	150,000	4
IA	50,000	66,000	81,659	68,923	80,000	177,448	9
ID	71,500	71,500	98,462	98,462	125,424	125,424	2
IL	46,000	62,650	107,086	96,000	125,914	239,500	12
IN	56,000	67,638	88,967	84,230	110,811	130,376	8
KS	34,000	51,000	88,887	67,261	145,000	168,800	6
KY	66,836	84,390	101,622	111,398	115,000	120,709	6
LA	49,979	51,681	79,486	70,415	93,487	138,010	7
MA	64,158	77,773	116,970	93,296	156,221	246,000	12

MD	62,395	68,646	97,840	103,750	120,850	127,650	6
ME	60,492	64,500	79,233	73,095	95,215	109,000	6
MI	45,720	60,000	107,639	90,399	110,314	331,200	11
MN	55,189	69,947	90,267	96,311	106,000	123,333	10
MO	47,500	61,673	96,485	73,174	121,727	220,000	11
MS	75,000	75,000	76,750	76,750	78,500	78,500	2
MT	42,000	48,500	79,050	77,500	109,600	119,200	4
NC	39,500	60,276	89,189	82,592	103,000	222,585	16
ND	52,955	56,655	69,971	59,040	67,506	119,775	10
NE	54,053	54,053	60,672	62,400	65,563	65,563	3
NH	211,725	211,725	211,725	211,725	211,725	211,725	1
NJ	61,000	88,910	107,119	108,633	125,000	151,031	10
NM	45,736	45,736	58,868	58,868	72,000	72,000	2
NV	63,492	63,492	115,505	84,500	198,523	198,523	3
NY	38,433	72,000	99,013	90,850	136,167	169,416	13
OH	41,000	50,454	85,672	78,132	119,629	161,650	12
OK	36,071	51,000	72,674	61,800	70,944	154,431	6
OR	54,014	72,007	83,579	90,150	95,150	100,000	4
PA	45,438	67,250	107,256	89,505	123,802	281,400	24
RI	58,000	58,000	73,500	73,500	89,000	89,000	2
SC	55,056	71,225	84,169	75,000	84,497	150,000	7
SD	68,963	68,963	75,884	75,884	82,804	82,804	2
TN	40,000	46,000	61,434	61,500	69,672	90,000	5
TX	39,150	61,500	77,292	68,800	87,200	197,062	27
UT	54,000	54,000	78,201	71,602	109,000	109,000	3
VA	59,245	82,000	116,993	110,857	130,384	240,000	12
VT	48,000	48,000	54,250	54,250	60,500	60,500	2
WA	60,000	64,000	74,571	74,173	83,191	90,614	11
WI	80,000	82,459	94,301	87,542	99,454	130,053	7
WV	54,363	54,363	54,806	54,806	55,248	55,248	2

DEPUTY/ASSOCIATE/ASSISTANT DIRECTOR

Persons who report to the Director and manage major aspects of the library operation (e.g., technical services, public services, collection development, systems/automation).
Two-Year College

Regional Data

	Min	Q1	Mean	Median	Q3	Max	N
North Atlantic	34,914	56,000	60,328	58,515	72,640	73,100	11
Great Lakes & Plains	40,000	49,000	57,987	57,000	64,586	81,500	9
Southeast	42,411	43,081	52,393	56,460	58,696	61,318	5
West & Southwest	36,000	49,140	60,764	58,524	75,044	90,987	19
ALL REGIONS	34,914	49,672	59,136	57,758	68,281	90,987	44

State Data

	Min	Q1	Mean	Median	Q3	Max	N
AZ	68,831	68,831	79,783	79,530	90,987	90,987	3
CA	74,050	74,050	76,927	77,022	79,710	79,710	3
CO	42,000	42,000	42,000	42,000	42,000	42,000	1

HI	75,044	75,044	75,044	75,044	75,044	75,044	1
IL	49,000	53,000	61,100	57,000	65,000	81,500	5
KS	40,000	40,000	40,000	40,000	40,000	40,000	1
MA	56,192	56,431	57,859	57,593	59,288	60,060	4
MD	34,914	34,914	34,914	34,914	34,914	34,914	1
MI	64,586	64,586	64,586	64,586	64,586	64,586	1
NC	56,460	56,460	58,825	58,696	61,318	61,318	3
NJ	56,000	67,730	68,494	72,640	73,000	73,100	5
NM	42,104	42,104	42,104	42,104	42,104	42,104	1
OH	48,800	48,800	55,900	55,900	63,000	63,000	2
OK	49,140	49,140	49,140	49,140	49,140	49,140	1
PA	54,782	54,782	54,782	54,782	54,782	54,782	1
SC	42,411	42,411	42,746	42,746	43,081	43,081	2
TX	36,000	36,000	48,614	47,077	62,766	62,766	3
WA	50,204	51,434	55,042	55,045	58,524	60,000	6

DEPUTY/ASSOCIATE/ASSISTANT DIRECTOR—CONTINUED

Four-Year College

Regional Data

	Min	Q1	Mean	Median	Q3	Max	N
North Atlantic	35,000	51,047	68,036	71,463	78,632	110,973	25
Great Lakes & Plains	37,900	48,100	56,019	55,876	63,296	81,300	17
Southeast	30,900	36,205	43,533	41,740	46,200	69,142	16
West & Southwest	33,000	47,555	50,794	52,240	55,715	61,810	9
ALL REGIONS	30,900	43,000	56,819	52,240	69,142	110,973	67

State Data

	Min	Q1	Mean	Median	Q3	Max	N
AR	48,000	48,000	48,000	48,000	48,000	48,000	1
CA	58,300	58,300	58,300	58,300	58,300	58,300	1
FL	30,900	33,765	35,565	35,525	37,677	40,000	6
IL	37,900	41,919	48,809	47,019	55,698	63,296	4
IN	43,000	43,000	43,000	43,000	43,000	43,000	1
MA	47,247	49,147	64,574	64,840	80,001	81,370	4
MD	71,163	71,163	71,163	71,163	71,163	71,163	1
ME	37,476	48,962	61,215	54,182	86,160	86,330	6
MN	39,100	58,376	60,119	62,938	67,655	69,706	6
MS	41,000	41,000	44,200	44,200	47,400	47,400	2
ND	55,876	55,876	55,876	55,876	55,876	55,876	1
NJ	35,000	35,000	82,461	101,410	110,973	110,973	3
NY	50,243	60,853	68,083	72,884	75,314	76,322	4
OH	49,482	50,068	60,553	55,716	71,039	81,300	4
OR	61,810	61,810	61,810	61,810	61,810	61,810	1
PA	47,000	51,180	69,203	71,600	75,771	104,686	7
SC	69,142	69,142	69,142	69,142	69,142	69,142	1
SD	55,285	55,285	55,285	55,285	55,285	55,285	1
TN	36,360	36,360	51,108	51,108	65,855	65,855	2
TX	33,000	43,000	48,148	50,000	55,524	55,715	7

VA	42,992	42,992	44,297	44,900	45,000	45,000	3
WV	42,480	42,480	42,480	42,480	42,480	42,480	1

DEPUTY/ASSOCIATE/ASSISTANT DIRECTOR—CONTINUED
University (includes ARL data)

Regional Data

	Min	Q1	Mean	Median	Q3	Max	N
North Atlantic	47,440	68,059	92,070	93,400	113,850	150,443	97
Great Lakes & Plains	33,000	68,734	84,570	81,897	98,000	155,592	89
Southeast	23,067	62,200	75,894	74,179	87,916	138,420	125
West & Southwest	41,000	77,826	95,639	93,991	116,366	165,670	92
ALL REGIONS	23,067	67,080	86,211	83,788	104,781	165,670	403

State Data

	Min	Q1	Mean	Median	Q3	Max	N
AL	42,678	67,080	76,567	83,589	90,640	102,100	11
AR	40,747	40,747	54,374	54,374	68,000	68,000	2
AZ	74,200	82,316	94,518	86,815	103,472	144,670	10
CA	78,036	106,725	114,336	116,366	122,842	161,200	34
CO	73,544	82,919	97,476	97,600	109,000	118,700	11
CT	54,421	55,459	71,307	68,059	82,750	95,847	5
DC	51,500	62,500	90,064	92,963	111,536	128,589	29
FL	52,042	67,577	79,770	83,406	89,038	112,270	29
GA	56,229	56,500	69,667	71,239	74,879	87,916	6
HI	115,200	115,200	115,200	115,200	115,200	115,200	1
IA	95,028	95,028	101,525	98,972	110,574	110,574	3
ID	73,528	73,528	75,276	75,276	77,023	77,023	2
IL	33,000	69,905	89,770	88,665	112,225	143,557	24
IN	60,000	72,064	76,536	74,829	84,586	89,332	8
KS	39,000	64,751	76,383	75,980	92,754	105,096	8
KY	45,000	65,930	69,712	69,434	75,432	82,068	14
LA	37,351	41,919	51,780	46,722	57,319	86,126	9
MA	51,960	79,944	97,450	107,578	117,350	120,290	6
MD	69,925	76,260	79,914	78,532	82,875	94,050	8
MI	48,000	61,658	98,466	82,600	144,478	155,592	5
MN	61,915	62,674	70,125	72,661	76,688	76,688	5
MO	50,076	72,132	87,483	90,565	99,358	122,923	24
MT	56,880	59,265	62,494	62,048	65,723	69,000	4
NC	40,820	60,324	79,038	75,199	91,393	138,420	24
ND	77,771	77,771	77,771	77,771	77,771	77,771	1
NH	113,850	113,850	118,488	118,440	123,125	123,221	4
NJ	92,370	100,000	108,193	108,965	119,617	122,568	10
NM	41,000	41,000	41,000	41,000	41,000	41,000	1
NV	142,788	142,788	142,788	142,788	142,788	142,788	1
NY	47,440	62,000	81,174	85,500	97,268	129,504	23
OH	63,895	66,335	73,204	69,210	80,206	90,236	8
OK	81,000	81,000	82,840	81,538	85,983	85,983	3
OR	56,751	59,160	64,532	62,796	67,627	78,060	6

PA	59,000	92,253	109,628	110,166	134,174	150,443	12
SC	71,522	71,522	71,522	71,522	71,522	71,522	2
TN	50,000	50,000	50,000	50,000	50,000	50,000	1
TX	49,415	53,000	81,216	74,983	95,608	165,670	14
UT	72,695	72,695	76,312	76,312	79,929	79,929	2
VA	44,346	68,047	86,514	84,238	103,116	129,600	26
WA	90,229	90,229	90,229	90,229	90,229	90,229	1
WI	69,226	69,226	79,459	80,867	88,285	88,285	3
WV	23,067	23,067	23,067	23,067	23,067	23,067	1

DEPUTY/ASSOCIATE/ASSISTANT DIRECTOR—CONTINUED
ALL ACADEMIC LIBRARIES

Regional Data

	Min	Q1	Mean	Median	Q3	Max	N
North Atlantic	34,914	62,000	84,927	82,750	106,923	150,443	133
Great Lakes & Plains	33,000	62,674	78,269	74,500	93,751	155,592	115
Southeast	23,067	53,319	71,542	68,548	86,987	138,420	146
West & Southwest	33,000	61,599	86,754	82,618	111,335	165,670	120
ALL REGIONS	23,067	60,089	80,062	76,490	97,600	165,670	514

State Data

	Min	Q1	Mean	Median	Q3	Max	N
AL	42,678	67,080	76,567	83,589	90,640	102,100	11
AR	40,747	40,747	52,249	48,000	68,000	68,000	3
AZ	68,831	80,481	91,118	84,815	92,722	144,670	13
CA	58,300	97,284	109,908	115,366	122,000	161,200	38
CO	42,000	82,060	92,853	96,900	107,175	118,700	12
CT	54,421	55,459	71,307	68,059	82,750	95,847	5
DC	51,500	62,500	90,064	92,963	111,536	128,589	29
FL	30,900	53,319	72,192	76,084	88,766	112,270	35
GA	56,229	56,500	69,667	71,239	74,879	87,916	6
HI	75,044	75,044	95,122	95,122	115,200	115,200	2
IA	95,028	95,028	101,525	98,972	110,574	110,574	3
ID	73,528	73,528	75,276	75,276	77,023	77,023	2
IL	33,000	60,978	80,461	76,226	106,582	143,557	33
IN	43,000	72,000	72,810	73,000	80,201	89,332	9
KS	39,000	64,640	72,340	75,900	89,131	105,096	9
KY	45,000	65,930	69,712	69,434	75,432	82,068	14
LA	37,351	41,919	51,780	46,722	57,319	86,126	9
MA	47,247	56,192	76,745	69,346	100,325	120,290	14
MD	34,914	71,163	74,539	77,631	80,000	94,050	10
ME	37,476	48,962	61,215	54,182	86,160	86,330	6
MI	48,000	61,658	92,819	73,593	144,478	155,592	6
MN	39,100	61,915	64,667	63,768	72,661	76,688	11
MO	50,076	72,132	87,483	90,565	99,358	122,923	24
MS	41,000	41,000	44,200	44,200	47,400	47,400	2
MT	56,880	59,265	62,494	62,048	65,723	69,000	4
NC	40,820	58,696	76,792	68,434	87,386	138,420	27

ND	55,876	55,876	66,824	66,824	77,771	77,771	2
NH	113,850	113,850	118,488	118,440	123,125	123,221	4
NJ	35,000	73,000	92,877	100,000	111,006	122,568	18
NM	41,000	41,000	41,552	41,552	42,104	42,104	2
NV	142,788	142,788	142,788	142,788	142,788	142,788	1
NY	47,440	62,000	79,234	76,322	94,553	129,504	27
OH	48,800	60,777	67,118	66,335	72,303	90,236	14
OK	49,140	65,070	74,415	81,269	83,761	85,983	4
OR	56,751	59,160	64,143	61,810	67,627	78,060	7
PA	47,000	60,500	92,737	92,253	122,712	150,443	20
SC	42,411	43,081	59,536	69,142	71,522	71,522	5
SD	55,285	55,285	55,285	55,285	55,285	55,285	1
TN	36,360	36,360	50,738	50,000	65,855	65,855	3
TX	33,000	49,708	67,496	55,620	78,058	165,670	24
UT	72,695	72,695	76,312	76,312	79,929	79,929	2
VA	42,992	63,800	82,147	81,800	100,600	129,600	29
WA	50,204	51,434	60,069	56,141	60,000	90,229	7
WI	69,226	69,226	79,459	80,867	88,285	88,285	3
WV	23,067	23,067	32,774	32,774	42,480	42,480	2

DEPARTMENT HEAD/BRANCH MANAGER/COORDINATOR

Persons who supervise one or more professional librarians.
Two-Year College

Regional Data

	Min	Q1	Mean	Median	Q3	Max	N
North Atlantic	49,088	51,954	68,098	63,559	84,242	96,185	4
Great Lakes & Plains	37,100	37,100	66,662	80,950	81,936	81,936	3
Southeast	38,000	44,922	48,072	47,414	52,679	58,000	6
West & Southwest	43,444	53,307	64,353	58,266	77,832	88,946	17
ALL REGIONS	37,100	46,800	61,827	54,910	77,832	96,185	30

State Data

	Min	Q1	Mean	Median	Q3	Max	N
AZ	88,946	88,946	88,946	88,946	88,946	88,946	1
CA	67,000	77,832	80,471	82,000	86,928	88,595	5
CO	43,444	43,444	44,283	44,283	45,122	45,122	2
GA	38,000	38,000	38,000	38,000	38,000	38,000	1
IL	80,950	80,950	81,443	81,443	81,936	81,936	2
LA	48,028	48,028	50,354	50,354	52,679	52,679	2
MO	37,100	37,100	37,100	37,100	37,100	37,100	1
NC	44,922	44,922	45,861	45,861	46,800	46,800	2
NJ	49,088	49,088	66,697	54,819	96,185	96,185	3
PA	72,299	72,299	72,299	72,299	72,299	72,299	1
TN	58,000	58,000	58,000	58,000	58,000	58,000	1
TX	46,314	53,307	59,091	55,000	72,648	73,999	7
WA	46,000	46,000	46,000	46,000	46,000	46,000	1
WY	54,500	54,500	54,500	54,500	54,500	54,500	1

DEPARTMENT HEAD/BRANCH MANAGER/COORDINATOR—CONTINUED
Four-Year College

Regional Data

	Min	Q1	Mean	Median	Q3	Max	N
North Atlantic	36,000	56,713	65,800	67,750	74,990	91,750	35
Great Lakes & Plains	27,000	47,200	58,205	53,462	74,295	78,899	11
Southeast	29,900	43,740	50,314	48,647	55,460	72,387	18
West & Southwest	29,900	33,648	43,593	43,770	48,980	62,700	16
ALL REGIONS	27,000	46,341	56,830	55,331	69,547	91,750	80

State Data

	Min	Q1	Mean	Median	Q3	Max	N
CA	60,500	60,500	61,600	61,600	62,700	62,700	2
FL	47,000	47,000	47,000	47,000	47,000	47,000	1
GA	40,000	40,000	40,000	40,000	40,000	40,000	1
IA	76,169	76,169	76,169	76,169	76,169	76,169	1
IN	47,200	47,200	47,200	47,200	47,200	47,200	1
KY	43,740	43,740	49,365	49,365	54,990	54,990	2
MA	41,546	56,200	65,808	67,750	71,717	91,750	13
ME	65,770	65,770	70,380	70,380	74,990	74,990	2
MN	53,462	53,462	63,608	67,655	69,706	69,706	3
NC	47,475	49,478	59,196	59,031	67,815	72,387	7
NJ	36,000	41,000	64,072	68,769	84,279	85,615	6
OH	27,000	46,299	54,344	49,786	74,295	78,899	6
OK	29,900	31,450	36,225	36,500	41,000	42,000	4
PA	54,240	59,990	65,879	65,777	71,600	78,121	14
SC	36,050	37,080	44,306	46,331	47,815	54,253	5
TN	29,900	29,900	42,012	42,012	54,124	54,124	2
TX	33,075	33,251	37,786	34,044	41,460	47,100	5
UT	45,540	45,540	47,921	47,610	50,612	50,612	3
WA	46,350	46,350	48,350	48,350	50,350	50,350	2

DEPARTMENT HEAD/BRANCH MANAGER/COORDINATOR—CONTINUED
University (includes ARL data)

Regional Data

	Min	Q1	Mean	Median	Q3	Max	N
North Atlantic	43,610	53,750	63,794	59,685	69,974	112,662	52
Great Lakes & Plains	37,273	52,132	61,940	59,755	68,206	112,164	94
Southeast	34,505	47,924	59,239	58,305	68,177	93,544	116
West & Southwest	38,947	57,814	67,967	64,916	76,411	109,487	66
ALL REGIONS	34,505	51,990	62,491	60,688	69,374	112,662	328

State Data

	Min	Q1	Mean	Median	Q3	Max	N
AR	34,505	44,020	45,688	46,313	49,490	52,848	9
AZ	61,882	61,882	69,631	69,063	77,947	77,947	3
CA	71,692	86,000	93,194	96,862	101,448	105,612	10

CO	60,704	75,709	76,016	77,000	78,167	88,498	5
CT	54,543	60,274	73,140	73,134	82,692	98,378	8
DC	50,200	51,600	61,279	53,750	70,958	87,415	4
FL	41,705	48,358	61,741	63,408	70,845	93,544	46
GA	43,590	47,795	56,028	56,083	64,260	68,354	4
ID	56,285	56,285	56,285	56,285	56,285	56,285	1
IL	72,176	90,746	95,952	91,246	107,900	112,164	9
IN	44,535	50,696	55,398	55,723	59,174	67,873	22
KS	65,590	65,590	65,590	65,590	65,590	65,590	1
KY	45,060	46,125	53,536	54,781	57,886	62,712	10
LA	40,000	49,483	53,870	52,061	63,303	63,748	9
MA	43,610	47,380	55,234	55,137	58,974	71,164	6
MD	46,000	53,500	60,225	60,147	68,440	72,000	12
ME	56,708	56,708	60,446	57,270	67,360	67,360	3
MI	41,600	45,255	52,162	53,308	58,224	61,280	6
MN	37,273	53,642	57,992	59,853	62,338	76,852	5
MO	43,434	60,111	64,297	68,206	69,252	82,422	13
MS	45,000	45,000	45,350	45,350	45,700	45,700	2
MT	58,992	65,134	66,211	67,607	68,831	70,491	5
NC	37,086	45,361	56,123	57,200	72,000	76,402	7
ND	59,000	60,136	63,266	60,514	67,984	68,694	5
NJ	100,682	100,682	100,682	100,682	100,682	100,682	1
NV	61,806	69,006	84,685	88,221	94,904	109,487	5
NY	58,190	59,208	77,340	69,947	86,694	112,662	5
OH	42,200	54,806	63,995	65,596	75,100	82,761	14
OR	40,284	40,284	40,284	40,284	40,284	40,284	1
PA	46,000	51,877	58,787	59,832	67,762	72,956	13
TX	38,947	50,955	58,387	60,395	66,140	76,411	26
UT	50,406	53,257	58,300	60,002	61,109	66,727	5
VA	39,330	59,285	65,262	67,600	72,800	81,571	29
WA	51,980	51,980	51,980	51,980	51,980	51,980	1
WI	45,992	47,335	53,864	52,722	59,753	65,693	19
WY	60,912	61,140	63,072	62,058	65,004	67,260	4

DEPARTMENT HEAD/BRANCH MANAGER/COORDINATOR—CONTINUED
ALL ACADEMIC LIBRARIES

Regional Data

	Min	Q1	Mean	Median	Q3	Max	N
North Atlantic	36,000	55,000	64,755	62,131	71,717	112,662	91
Great Lakes & Plains	27,000	50,958	61,691	59,755	68,683	112,164	108
Southeast	29,900	46,977	57,613	56,000	67,097	93,544	140
West & Southwest	29,900	50,406	63,407	61,806	73,999	109,487	99
ALL REGIONS	27,000	50,406	61,412	59,885	69,733	112,662	438

State Data

	Min	Q1	Mean	Median	Q3	Max	N
AR	34,505	44,020	45,688	46,313	49,490	52,848	9
AZ	61,882	65,473	74,460	73,505	83,447	88,946	4
CA	60,500	77,008	85,735	86,928	100,928	105,612	17

CO	43,444	45,122	66,949	75,709	78,167	88,498	7
CT	54,543	60,274	73,140	73,134	82,692	98,378	8
DC	50,200	51,600	61,279	53,750	70,958	87,415	4
FL	41,705	47,953	61,428	63,036	70,845	93,544	47
GA	38,000	40,000	50,352	47,795	60,166	68,354	6
IA	76,169	76,169	76,169	76,169	76,169	76,169	1
ID	56,285	56,285	56,285	56,285	56,285	56,285	1
IL	72,176	81,936	93,314	91,162	107,900	112,164	11
IN	44,535	49,633	55,042	55,122	59,174	67,873	23
KS	65,590	65,590	65,590	65,590	65,590	65,590	1
KY	43,740	45,963	52,841	54,276	57,827	62,712	12
LA	40,000	48,028	53,231	52,061	63,303	63,748	11
MA	41,546	53,431	62,469	58,974	71,164	91,750	19
MD	46,000	53,500	60,225	60,147	68,440	72,000	12
ME	56,708	57,270	64,420	65,770	67,360	74,990	5
MI	41,600	45,255	52,162	53,308	58,224	61,280	6
MN	37,273	53,552	60,098	61,096	68,681	76,852	8
MO	37,100	53,000	62,354	66,091	69,252	82,422	14
MS	45,000	45,000	45,350	45,350	45,700	45,700	2
MT	58,992	65,134	66,211	67,607	68,831	70,491	5
NC	37,086	46,388	56,184	56,330	65,269	76,402	16
ND	59,000	60,136	63,266	60,514	67,984	68,694	5
NJ	36,000	49,088	68,521	68,769	85,615	100,682	10
NV	61,806	69,006	84,685	88,221	94,904	109,487	5
NY	58,190	59,208	77,340	69,947	86,694	112,662	5
OH	27,000	47,487	61,100	63,574	74,869	82,761	20
OK	29,900	31,450	36,225	36,500	41,000	42,000	4
OR	40,284	40,284	40,284	40,284	40,284	40,284	1
PA	46,000	55,229	62,815	61,900	70,532	78,121	28
SC	36,050	37,080	44,306	46,331	47,815	54,253	5
TN	29,900	29,900	47,341	54,124	58,000	58,000	3
TX	33,075	47,000	55,806	56,293	64,698	76,411	38
UT	45,540	49,008	54,408	51,935	60,556	66,727	8
VA	39,330	59,285	65,262	67,600	72,800	81,571	29
WA	46,000	46,175	48,670	48,350	51,165	51,980	4
WI	45,992	47,335	53,864	52,722	59,753	65,693	19
WY	54,500	60,912	61,358	61,368	62,748	67,260	5

MANAGER/SUPERVISOR OF SUPPORT STAFF

Persons who supervise support staff in any part of the library but do not supervise professional librarians.
 Two-Year College

Regional Data

	Min	Q1	Mean	Median	Q3	Max	N
North Atlantic	36,400	36,400	57,425	57,425	78,450	78,450	2
Great Lakes & Plains	37,022	41,504	54,414	52,250	61,959	81,500	6
Southeast	34,500	43,919	46,986	46,449	52,700	55,254	8
West & Southwest	28,000	47,000	59,388	59,086	71,070	93,621	26
ALL REGIONS	28,000	44,508	56,221	54,226	67,536	93,621	42

	Min	Q1	Mean	Median	Q3	Max	N
AZ	67,034	67,034	70,517	70,517	74,000	74,000	2
CA	52,223	52,223	74,494	77,637	93,621	93,621	3
FL	47,039	47,039	47,039	47,039	47,039	47,039	1
IL	61,959	61,959	71,730	71,730	81,500	81,500	2
KS	46,500	46,500	46,500	46,500	46,500	46,500	1
LA	42,000	42,000	43,919	43,919	45,838	45,838	2
MA	36,400	36,400	36,400	36,400	36,400	36,400	1
NC	34,500	34,500	44,802	45,858	54,048	54,048	3
ND	37,022	37,022	39,263	39,263	41,504	41,504	2
NY	78,450	78,450	78,450	78,450	78,450	78,450	1
OH	58,000	58,000	58,000	58,000	58,000	58,000	1
SC	51,352	51,352	53,303	53,303	55,254	55,254	2
TX	32,495	44,508	57,528	57,416	68,778	87,488	19
UT	28,000	28,000	28,000	28,000	28,000	28,000	1
WA	58,524	58,524	58,524	58,524	58,524	58,524	1

MANAGER/SUPERVISOR OF SUPPORT STAFF—CONTINUED
Four-Year College

Regional Data

	Min	Q1	Mean	Median	Q3	Max	N
North Atlantic	32,000	47,740	54,242	53,846	59,988	93,968	38
Great Lakes & Plains	25,000	39,299	49,964	46,788	60,834	69,706	34
Southeast	30,406	39,103	46,985	47,000	54,346	65,200	26
West & Southwest	35,300	41,915	45,350	45,230	48,897	57,200	24
ALL REGIONS	25,000	42,120	49,754	48,247	57,155	93,968	122

State Data

	Min	Q1	Mean	Median	Q3	Max	N
AL	30,406	34,580	42,703	43,970	50,827	52,466	4
AR	36,579	36,579	36,890	36,890	37,200	37,200	2
CA	44,700	44,700	51,300	52,000	57,200	57,200	3
FL	38,700	40,100	48,100	44,250	56,100	65,200	4
GA	39,103	39,103	44,855	43,554	51,907	51,907	3
IA	43,000	45,000	52,647	52,000	56,689	66,548	5
ID	38,400	38,700	42,650	41,350	46,600	49,500	4
IL	25,000	25,000	25,000	25,000	25,000	25,000	1
IN	38,350	38,350	40,982	38,889	45,706	45,706	3
KY	40,000	40,000	40,000	40,000	40,000	40,000	1
MA	45,642	52,343	55,917	56,865	59,719	64,602	12
ME	35,603	35,603	49,044	55,470	56,060	56,060	3
MN	33,067	34,900	48,737	47,225	62,107	69,706	7
NC	42,120	48,542	52,996	54,391	58,562	61,240	9
NE	41,500	41,500	47,420	47,420	53,339	53,339	2
NJ	54,590	54,590	78,510	86,973	93,968	93,968	3
NY	32,000	36,500	41,351	42,665	46,202	48,074	4
OH	37,895	53,168	57,623	60,826	63,153	68,043	12

OK	35,300	35,300	38,500	36,000	44,200	44,200	3
OR	46,250	46,250	46,875	46,875	47,500	47,500	2
PA	44,777	47,740	53,843	51,051	61,965	63,978	15
SC	47,000	47,000	50,673	50,673	54,346	54,346	2
SD	38,192	38,192	38,864	39,100	39,299	39,299	3
TX	37,630	40,095	42,160	42,780	44,225	45,449	4
UT	47,610	47,610	50,131	50,612	52,170	52,170	3
VA	31,733	31,733	31,733	31,733	31,733	31,733	1
VT	34,500	34,500	34,500	34,500	34,500	34,500	1
WA	41,270	45,010	47,123	45,835	48,293	55,208	5
WI	43,540	43,540	43,540	43,540	43,540	43,540	1

MANAGER/SUPERVISOR OF SUPPORT STAFF—CONTINUED
University (includes ARL data)

Regional Data

	Min	Q1	Mean	Median	Q3	Max	N
North Atlantic	30,888	50,949	60,736	59,555	68,000	110,129	70
Great Lakes & Plains	26,000	44,525	51,625	50,175	58,344	80,532	114
Southeast	31,906	45,410	52,108	51,386	57,045	86,980	152
West & Southwest	33,333	48,845	62,418	55,022	73,635	117,000	87
ALL REGIONS	26,000	45,993	55,526	52,938	61,483	117,000	423

State Data

	Min	Q1	Mean	Median	Q3	Max	N
AL	46,654	49,796	63,154	60,462	76,511	85,037	4
AR	36,341	39,926	44,950	44,324	49,785	55,194	8
AZ	51,663	52,000	55,728	53,474	54,614	66,890	5
CA	40,673	75,822	87,971	92,124	102,698	117,000	20
CO	51,000	59,873	65,890	66,311	72,037	77,000	7
CT	53,915	60,478	66,770	63,952	72,726	82,618	9
DC	48,000	48,700	60,357	51,500	70,662	94,859	7
FL	38,820	47,231	53,665	53,010	60,499	82,000	51
GA	34,165	47,757	50,803	50,012	55,587	69,129	16
HI	45,213	45,213	45,213	45,213	45,213	45,213	1
IA	40,000	40,000	40,000	40,000	40,000	40,000	1
ID	49,712	49,712	56,285	56,285	62,858	62,858	2
IL	40,600	43,646	53,538	50,622	62,860	69,192	11
IN	37,965	41,127	44,457	42,122	48,500	56,631	13
KS	48,144	48,144	50,735	48,320	55,740	55,740	3
KY	33,000	49,524	51,430	52,956	54,928	59,739	25
LA	37,351	40,966	46,640	46,722	50,842	57,319	5
MA	40,915	40,915	51,217	53,761	58,974	58,974	3
MD	41,954	52,452	53,692	54,006	57,029	60,610	8
ME	30,888	30,888	31,311	31,262	31,782	31,782	3
MI	44,525	46,125	50,835	47,188	55,975	60,363	5
MN	37,688	44,808	54,386	52,850	66,897	70,141	14
MO	26,000	43,882	51,115	49,988	57,758	75,714	24
MS	36,600	37,000	37,800	37,400	38,200	39,800	5

MT	38,625	43,605	55,928	57,007	68,831	70,491	6
NC	31,906	39,668	49,867	45,276	54,870	86,980	20
ND	33,086	33,086	44,468	49,154	51,164	51,164	3
NE	47,759	47,759	49,108	49,108	50,456	50,456	2
NJ	50,949	62,706	76,437	71,084	93,968	104,039	9
NV	73,635	78,811	90,176	91,550	101,542	103,970	4
NY	45,060	61,204	64,625	66,160	68,000	78,100	10
OH	44,216	52,750	58,014	59,885	61,420	80,532	17
OR	33,333	33,333	33,333	33,333	33,333	33,333	1
PA	38,546	44,958	57,941	58,500	64,558	110,129	21
TN	44,392	44,392	55,233	55,233	66,074	66,074	2
TX	36,029	42,290	47,282	48,000	52,419	59,749	31
UT	50,129	50,255	56,081	53,769	61,908	66,658	4
VA	48,060	53,469	58,914	58,393	63,032	73,045	16
WA	51,965	51,965	53,793	53,793	55,620	55,620	2
WI	41,362	45,993	50,761	49,276	54,486	65,452	21

MANAGER/SUPERVISOR OF SUPPORT STAFF—CONTINUED
ALL ACADEMIC LIBRARIES

Regional Data

	Min	Q1	Mean	Median	Q3	Max	N
North Atlantic	30,888	48,700	58,432	57,974	64,363	110,129	110
Great Lakes & Plains	25,000	43,540	51,367	49,988	59,985	81,500	154
Southeast	30,406	44,314	51,171	50,524	56,200	86,980	186
West & Southwest	28,000	45,010	58,853	52,419	68,778	117,000	137
ALL REGIONS	25,000	44,958	54,376	52,000	60,834	117,000	587

State Data

	Min	Q1	Mean	Median	Q3	Max	N
AL	30,406	42,704	52,928	50,827	60,462	85,037	8
AR	36,341	37,200	43,338	41,911	48,198	55,194	10
AZ	51,663	52,000	59,954	54,614	67,034	74,000	7
CA	40,673	65,000	82,184	85,020	102,204	117,000	26
CO	51,000	59,873	65,890	66,311	72,037	77,000	7
CT	53,915	60,478	66,770	63,952	72,726	82,618	9
DC	48,000	48,700	60,357	51,500	70,662	94,859	7
FL	38,700	46,977	53,149	50,705	60,223	82,000	56
GA	34,165	43,554	49,864	49,818	54,860	69,129	19
HI	45,213	45,213	45,213	45,213	45,213	45,213	1
IA	40,000	43,000	50,540	48,500	56,689	66,548	6
ID	38,400	39,000	47,195	46,600	49,712	62,858	6
IL	25,000	43,646	54,098	54,483	62,860	81,500	14
IN	37,965	40,955	43,805	41,851	47,103	56,631	16
KS	46,500	47,322	49,676	48,232	52,030	55,740	4
KY	33,000	48,000	50,991	52,758	54,928	59,739	26
LA	37,351	40,966	45,863	45,838	50,842	57,319	7
MA	36,400	50,743	53,816	54,500	59,212	64,602	16
MD	41,954	52,452	53,692	54,006	57,029	60,610	8

ME	30,888	31,262	40,178	33,693	55,470	56,060	6
MI	44,525	46,125	50,835	47,188	55,975	60,363	5
MN	33,067	42,240	52,503	50,349	63,836	70,141	21
MO	26,000	43,882	51,115	49,988	57,758	75,714	24
MS	36,600	37,000	37,800	37,400	38,200	39,800	5
MT	38,625	43,605	55,928	57,007	68,831	70,491	6
NC	31,906	41,830	50,272	47,058	55,198	86,980	32
ND	33,086	37,022	42,386	41,504	49,154	51,164	5
NE	41,500	44,630	48,264	49,108	51,898	53,339	4
NJ	50,949	61,133	76,955	73,229	93,968	104,039	12
NV	73,635	78,811	90,176	91,550	101,542	103,970	4
NY	32,000	45,060	59,340	61,517	68,000	78,450	15
OH	37,895	52,750	57,857	60,116	62,171	80,532	30
OK	35,300	35,300	38,500	36,000	44,200	44,200	3
OR	33,333	33,333	42,361	46,250	47,500	47,500	3
PA	38,546	47,250	56,234	57,142	62,393	110,129	36
SC	47,000	49,176	51,988	52,849	54,800	55,254	4
SD	38,192	38,192	38,864	39,100	39,299	39,299	3
TN	44,392	44,392	55,233	55,233	66,074	66,074	2
TX	32,495	42,559	50,508	48,860	55,000	87,488	54
UT	28,000	48,870	50,340	50,496	54,664	66,658	8
VA	31,733	52,597	57,315	57,500	63,000	73,045	17
VT	34,500	34,500	34,500	34,500	34,500	34,500	1
WA	41,270	45,423	50,216	50,129	55,414	58,524	8
WI	41,362	45,993	50,433	48,353	54,486	65,452	22

LIBRARIAN WHO DOES NOT SUPERVISE

Full-time staff with master's degrees from programs in library and information studies accredited by the ALA who was not reported earlier and who does not supervise.
Two-Year College

Regional Data

	Min	Q1	Mean	Median	Q3	Max	N
North Atlantic	31,554	37,856	54,364	48,747	63,174	96,000	18
Great Lakes & Plains	34,521	56,626	65,309	67,554	76,481	87,911	12
Southeast	28,881	40,819	49,780	46,358	53,614	84,295	30
West & Southwest	30,610	43,894	57,414	54,769	70,133	91,086	88
ALL REGIONS	28,881	43,031	56,136	53,595	67,600	96,000	148

State Data

	Min	Q1	Mean	Median	Q3	Max	N
AZ	53,721	55,655	69,302	73,379	78,442	88,946	13
CA	45,126	65,992	75,599	76,600	85,773	91,086	17
CO	38,500	38,500	40,972	40,972	43,444	43,444	2
CT	59,931	59,931	73,924	73,924	87,917	87,917	2
FL	43,123	53,614	58,219	55,990	67,199	71,170	5
GA	40,000	42,676	47,481	46,850	52,286	56,223	4
HI	60,972	60,972	62,712	62,712	64,452	64,452	2
IA	66,000	66,000	66,000	66,000	66,000	66,000	1

IL	69,108	69,108	69,108	69,108	69,108	69,108	1
KS	34,521	34,521	50,240	46,500	69,700	69,700	3
LA	40,819	40,819	40,819	40,819	40,819	40,819	1
MD	31,554	31,554	34,137	34,137	36,719	36,719	2
MI	73,931	73,931	81,828	83,641	87,911	87,911	3
MO	53,719	56,626	63,099	59,823	69,572	79,030	4
NC	40,320	40,500	43,674	41,976	47,732	50,138	7
NJ	37,856	45,000	59,950	54,667	73,055	96,000	10
NV	51,237	53,207	58,113	58,309	63,019	64,597	4
NY	37,200	37,200	44,058	44,058	50,916	50,916	2
OK	34,945	34,945	37,823	36,590	41,935	41,935	3
PA	35,000	35,000	37,412	37,412	39,824	39,824	2
SC	28,881	43,260	53,349	50,470	69,637	84,295	11
TN	34,000	34,000	39,500	39,500	45,000	45,000	2
TX	30,610	38,917	48,308	45,170	54,360	85,200	34
WA	34,072	48,000	51,583	51,816	56,000	66,000	13

LIBRARIAN WHO DOES NOT SUPERVISE—CONTINUED
Four-Year College

Regional Data

	Min	Q1	Mean	Median	Q3	Max	N
North Atlantic	30,315	43,028	51,857	50,368	58,851	100,682	84
Great Lakes & Plains	31,000	37,500	44,716	42,000	50,855	65,178	37
Southeast	31,108	37,447	41,562	40,283	46,849	55,012	38
West & Southwest	31,471	37,100	43,726	46,058	48,608	52,000	22
ALL REGIONS	30,315	38,400	47,248	46,600	53,040	100,682	181

State Data

	Min	Q1	Mean	Median	Q3	Max	N
AL	37,671	37,671	39,609	40,578	40,578	40,578	3
AR	33,200	33,200	33,200	33,200	33,200	33,200	1
CA	47,000	47,000	49,583	50,500	51,250	51,250	3
CO	52,000	52,000	52,000	52,000	52,000	52,000	1
DE	36,000	36,000	36,000	36,000	36,000	36,000	1
FL	46,000	46,000	46,500	46,500	47,000	47,000	2
GA	36,403	37,753	40,228	40,093	42,704	44,325	4
IA	34,977	37,015	42,721	41,599	49,000	53,881	12
IL	43,193	43,193	43,193	43,193	43,193	43,193	1
IN	36,500	41,000	49,758	50,189	56,878	65,178	9
KY	34,680	36,340	40,088	38,935	43,835	47,800	4
MA	30,315	42,500	49,504	48,400	55,576	73,087	23
MD	49,999	51,146	56,316	53,041	61,486	69,183	4
ME	36,500	45,000	46,882	46,438	48,220	58,250	5
MI	33,000	33,000	33,000	33,000	33,000	33,000	1
MN	38,074	38,074	44,516	39,300	56,175	56,175	3
MO	32,970	32,970	36,085	33,336	41,949	41,949	3
MS	38,000	38,000	38,000	38,000	38,000	38,000	1
NC	37,500	41,550	46,201	45,980	51,019	55,012	8

NE	52,478	52,478	52,478	52,478	52,478	52,478	1
NJ	31,000	37,000	58,241	52,896	66,774	100,682	11
NY	41,704	50,339	52,391	52,128	57,434	60,349	5
OH	31,000	36,190	46,221	49,588	55,185	55,400	7
OK	31,471	31,524	34,162	34,038	36,800	37,100	4
OR	36,100	38,850	43,571	42,825	48,300	51,780	5
PA	33,400	43,200	52,528	54,789	61,579	72,657	34
SC	35,000	36,446	41,929	40,565	46,849	52,812	9
TN	33,530	33,530	42,398	42,398	51,266	51,266	2
TX	36,300	36,300	39,768	41,004	42,000	42,000	3
UT	45,540	46,575	47,987	48,447	48,608	50,766	5
VA	31,108	34,020	35,823	37,216	37,625	37,750	4
VT	33,200	33,200	33,200	33,200	33,200	33,200	1
WA	47,488	47,488	47,488	47,488	47,488	47,488	1

LIBRARIAN WHO DOES NOT SUPERVISE—CONTINUED
University (includes ARL data)

Regional Data

	Min	Q1	Mean	Median	Q3	Max	N
North Atlantic	27,180	47,830	58,035	55,412	64,173	122,620	449
Great Lakes & Plains	30,000	43,903	51,828	49,050	56,988	95,477	514
Southeast	29,994	45,353	52,434	51,496	58,209	116,865	459
West & Southwest	26,246	46,572	59,553	55,472	68,352	106,620	437
ALL REGIONS	26,246	45,575	55,293	52,700	61,500	122,620	1,859

State Data

	Min	Q1	Mean	Median	Q3	Max	N
AL	37,620	50,100	56,760	53,451	65,590	86,681	59
AR	29,994	29,994	35,026	33,657	41,428	41,428	3
AZ	46,572	52,531	58,838	57,129	64,743	97,893	48
CA	42,204	60,486	73,565	73,356	85,740	106,620	156
CO	26,246	47,708	51,831	52,991	57,434	63,993	35
CT	34,086	50,001	56,696	57,000	64,363	82,750	13
DC	42,750	50,098	57,945	57,538	62,068	84,460	58
FL	35,360	44,000	50,073	49,612	56,248	66,957	107
GA	32,142	42,700	48,982	47,098	56,581	67,316	23
HI	36,840	45,391	59,437	59,357	69,721	86,502	26
IA	33,415	44,540	50,712	49,333	56,396	73,569	26
ID	44,013	44,669	51,161	48,808	53,810	70,700	8
IL	36,889	46,783	55,938	53,071	63,370	93,030	116
IN	39,520	41,052	45,718	44,863	48,656	59,017	31
KS	32,505	41,056	48,289	45,500	53,137	79,644	37
KY	35,000	41,856	47,858	46,809	53,448	65,737	26
LA	33,000	40,317	44,201	41,960	47,792	67,520	16
MA	36,138	53,160	64,489	61,377	76,246	120,820	68
MD	40,000	46,200	51,878	51,493	55,412	84,475	22
ME	33,155	35,681	40,307	43,539	44,290	44,872	5
MI	34,671	44,173	54,070	50,883	61,218	87,489	84

MN	40,046	47,624	57,848	56,781	62,929	95,477	43
MO	30,000	42,701	47,748	47,544	50,508	75,714	82
MT	39,140	41,577	47,692	45,985	51,811	65,000	13
NC	32,000	48,679	55,669	54,000	61,000	116,865	102
ND	38,000	41,662	45,708	47,151	48,040	54,094	11
NE	39,500	39,500	43,428	40,560	50,224	50,224	3
NH	43,285	51,324	58,310	58,371	63,746	80,000	25
NJ	39,129	53,154	70,427	64,390	88,644	122,620	37
NV	74,662	76,088	79,070	77,995	79,352	87,252	5
NY	37,132	49,471	59,168	56,030	66,964	108,820	102
OH	34,000	41,246	50,302	47,933	55,557	93,612	59
OK	27,413	43,785	47,517	49,681	50,916	56,383	24
OR	38,628	38,628	50,289	54,646	57,593	57,593	3
PA	27,180	44,374	51,923	50,949	59,172	84,454	116
SC	35,020	41,200	48,214	46,611	53,195	87,273	34
TN	39,863	39,863	41,682	41,682	43,500	43,500	2
TX	35,000	41,913	47,631	45,673	53,076	78,279	59
UT	36,225	37,290	40,151	39,271	43,743	46,536	14
VA	40,500	48,600	54,902	54,652	59,517	82,000	87
VT	35,000	35,000	36,667	35,000	40,000	40,000	3
WA	37,355	41,300	50,954	50,977	55,880	72,070	31
WI	40,125	45,994	49,218	52,208	53,157	58,940	22

LIBRARIAN WHO DOES NOT SUPERVISE—CONTINUED
ALL ACADEMIC LIBRARIES

Regional Data

	Min	Q1	Mean	Median	Q3	Max	N
North Atlantic	27,180	46,971	56,973	54,750	63,095	122,620	551
Great Lakes & Plains	30,000	43,451	51,648	49,030	56,967	95,477	563
Southeast	28,881	43,949	51,499	50,607	57,000	116,865	527
West & Southwest	26,246	45,477	58,573	54,744	66,882	106,620	547
ALL REGIONS	26,246	45,000	54,684	52,052	61,197	122,620	2,188

State Data

	Min	Q1	Mean	Median	Q3	Max	N
AL	37,620	48,981	55,930	52,670	64,806	86,681	62
AR	29,994	31,597	34,570	33,429	37,543	41,428	4
AZ	46,572	53,261	61,068	57,652	66,815	97,893	61
CA	42,204	60,486	73,352	73,356	85,740	106,620	176
CO	26,246	47,500	51,264	52,092	57,044	63,993	38
CT	34,086	50,001	58,993	57,682	73,249	87,917	15
DC	42,750	50,098	57,945	57,538	62,068	84,460	58
DE	36,000	36,000	36,000	36,000	36,000	36,000	1
FL	35,360	44,867	50,367	49,806	56,248	71,170	114
GA	32,142	40,247	47,659	45,362	54,222	67,316	31
HI	36,840	47,074	59,671	61,224	69,180	86,502	28
IA	33,415	41,198	48,645	47,956	53,881	73,569	39
ID	44,013	44,669	51,161	48,808	53,810	70,700	8

IL	36,889	46,566	55,942	53,071	63,440	93,030	118
IN	36,500	41,052	46,627	45,256	49,996	65,178	40
KS	32,505	41,028	48,435	45,866	53,176	79,644	40
KY	34,680	40,365	46,822	46,297	52,020	65,737	30
LA	33,000	40,633	44,002	41,919	44,741	67,520	17
MA	30,315	48,400	60,701	58,120	69,905	120,820	91
MD	31,554	45,045	51,244	51,493	55,399	84,475	28
ME	33,155	36,500	43,595	44,581	46,438	58,250	10
MI	33,000	44,173	54,777	51,561	62,893	87,911	88
MN	38,074	47,509	56,978	56,693	62,744	95,477	46
MO	30,000	42,332	48,045	47,561	51,714	79,030	89
MS	38,000	38,000	38,000	38,000	38,000	38,000	1
MT	39,140	41,577	47,692	45,985	51,811	65,000	13
NC	32,000	47,486	54,304	52,782	59,000	116,865	117
ND	38,000	41,662	45,708	47,151	48,040	54,094	11
NE	39,500	40,030	45,691	45,392	51,351	52,478	4
NH	43,285	51,324	58,310	58,371	63,746	80,000	25
NJ	31,000	49,233	66,310	60,301	82,821	122,620	58
NV	51,237	61,440	69,756	74,662	77,995	87,252	9
NY	37,132	49,471	58,580	55,760	65,000	108,820	109
OH	31,000	41,246	49,869	47,967	55,323	93,612	66
OK	27,413	41,202	44,855	45,603	50,823	56,383	31
OR	36,100	38,739	46,090	45,563	53,213	57,593	8
PA	27,180	43,494	51,867	51,411	59,599	84,454	152
SC	28,881	40,170	48,213	46,355	53,195	87,273	54
TN	33,530	34,000	41,193	41,682	45,000	51,266	6
TX	30,610	41,158	47,625	45,249	53,139	85,200	96
UT	36,225	37,308	42,213	41,200	46,536	50,766	19
VA	31,108	48,400	54,063	54,125	59,000	82,000	91
VT	33,200	34,100	35,800	35,000	37,500	40,000	4
WA	34,072	43,105	51,059	51,000	55,880	72,070	45
WI	40,125	45,994	49,218	52,208	53,157	58,940	22

BEGINNING LIBRARIAN

Full-time staff hired in the last six months with master's degrees from programs in library and information studies accredited by the ALA, but with no professional experience after receiving the degree.
Two-Year College

Regional Data

	Min	Q1	Mean	Median	Q3	Max	N
North Atlantic	30,000	33,422	41,928	43,467	46,791	54,424	6
Great Lakes & Plains	34,000	41,000	48,721	47,183	54,039	68,923	6
Southeast	24,710	33,914	35,922	36,718	38,016	51,216	10
West & Southwest	36,000	45,948	60,440	54,109	82,762	91,086	22
ALL REGIONS	24,710	37,715	50,745	46,370	57,212	91,086	44

State Data

	Min	Q1	Mean	Median	Q3	Max	N
CA	54,294	76,600	79,602	83,991	88,041	91,086	9
CO	36,000	36,000	36,750	36,750	37,500	37,500	2
CT	54,424	54,424	54,424	54,424	54,424	54,424	1
FL	24,710	26,000	34,785	35,000	37,000	51,216	5
GA	39,000	39,000	39,000	39,000	39,000	39,000	1
IA	68,923	68,923	68,923	68,923	68,923	68,923	1
IL	41,000	41,000	41,000	41,000	41,000	41,000	1
KS	34,000	34,000	34,000	34,000	34,000	34,000	1
MA	44,500	44,500	44,500	44,500	44,500	44,500	1
MI	44,686	44,686	49,468	49,679	54,039	54,039	3
NC	33,914	35,175	36,574	37,183	37,973	38,016	4
NM	39,428	39,428	39,428	39,428	39,428	39,428	1
NV	45,948	45,948	45,948	45,948	45,948	45,948	1
NY	30,000	30,000	36,738	33,422	46,791	46,791	3
PA	42,433	42,433	42,433	42,433	42,433	42,433	1
TX	39,500	40,428	50,542	48,784	60,000	64,000	5
UT	48,000	48,000	48,000	48,000	48,000	48,000	1
WA	48,936	48,936	51,225	50,814	53,924	53,924	3

BEGINNING LIBRARIAN—CONTINUED
Four-Year College

Regional Data

	Min	Q1	Mean	Median	Q3	Max	N
North Atlantic	33,400	38,750	40,800	40,500	43,250	48,000	8
Great Lakes & Plains	35,000	36,000	45,274	40,000	49,654	90,431	11
Southeast	30,000	30,768	39,215	36,750	40,365	80,776	14
West & Southwest	29,000	29,500	33,375	32,500	37,250	39,500	4
ALL REGIONS	29,000	35,000	40,728	39,500	41,500	90,431	37

State Data

	Min	Q1	Mean	Median	Q3	Max	N
CO	35,000	35,000	35,000	35,000	35,000	35,000	1
FL	35,000	35,000	35,000	35,000	35,000	35,000	1
GA	30,000	30,000	35,000	35,000	40,000	40,000	2
IA	40,000	40,000	41,750	41,750	43,500	43,500	2
IL	37,000	37,000	37,000	37,000	37,000	37,000	1
LA	30,000	30,000	30,000	30,000	30,000	30,000	2
MA	40,000	40,000	42,500	42,500	45,000	45,000	2
MI	36,000	36,000	38,000	38,000	40,000	40,000	2
MN	49,654	49,654	50,042	50,042	50,429	50,429	2
MS	36,500	40,365	48,648	42,752	42,849	80,776	5
MT	30,000	30,000	30,000	30,000	30,000	30,000	1
NC	33,000	33,000	35,000	35,000	37,000	37,000	2
ND	36,000	36,000	36,000	36,000	36,000	36,000	1
NJ	41,500	41,500	41,500	41,500	41,500	41,500	1
OH	35,000	35,000	62,716	62,716	90,431	90,431	2

OK	29,000	29,000	29,000	29,000	29,000	29,000	1
PA	33,400	38,000	39,980	39,500	41,000	48,000	5
SD	40,000	40,000	40,000	40,000	40,000	40,000	1
VA	40,000	40,000	40,000	40,000	40,000	40,000	1
WA	39,500	39,500	39,500	39,500	39,500	39,500	1
WV	30,768	30,768	30,768	30,768	30,768	30,768	1

BEGINNING LIBRARIAN—CONTINUED
University (includes ARL data)

Regional Data

	Min	Q1	Mean	Median	Q3	Max	N
North Atlantic	30,000	40,000	43,796	43,050	48,958	56,000	43
Great Lakes & Plains	25,000	38,000	40,964	40,675	44,500	60,030	50
Southeast	30,000	38,500	44,812	41,000	50,256	77,314	33
West & Southwest	35,000	40,025	48,616	43,008	54,099	97,582	40
ALL REGIONS	25,000	39,000	44,307	42,008	48,000	97,582	166

State Data

	Min	Q1	Mean	Median	Q3	Max	N
AL	37,992	37,992	37,992	37,992	37,992	37,992	1
AR	37,000	37,000	38,000	38,000	39,000	39,000	2
AZ	38,000	43,000	46,912	44,908	48,723	61,932	6
CA	40,008	42,204	58,598	55,944	66,512	97,582	15
CO	42,000	42,000	45,417	42,000	52,250	52,250	3
CT	48,958	48,958	48,958	48,958	48,958	48,958	1
DC	41,000	45,600	48,692	49,000	54,000	56,000	13
FL	40,000	40,000	41,400	40,000	43,000	44,000	5
GA	35,000	41,000	50,869	50,101	53,781	77,314	10
HI	35,964	35,964	40,218	40,218	44,472	44,472	2
IA	30,282	31,200	32,813	31,200	31,200	41,795	6
ID	42,016	42,016	42,516	42,516	43,015	43,015	2
IL	33,000	42,434	44,138	44,500	46,000	57,000	13
IN	37,000	37,500	41,000	39,500	44,500	48,000	4
KS	31,413	38,790	40,735	39,943	43,000	51,000	8
KY	30,000	30,000	30,000	30,000	30,000	30,000	1
LA	32,000	32,000	40,947	40,000	50,842	50,842	3
MA	40,730	40,730	44,633	45,076	47,647	50,810	7
MD	34,800	35,700	41,417	40,500	47,000	50,000	6
ME	43,539	43,539	43,539	43,539	43,539	43,539	1
MI	39,000	40,500	46,008	42,500	51,515	60,030	4
MN	51,000	51,000	52,898	52,898	54,795	54,795	2
MO	35,875	35,875	38,125	38,500	40,000	40,000	3
MT	43,000	43,000	43,000	43,000	43,000	43,000	1
NC	42,000	42,000	54,871	54,871	67,742	67,742	2
ND	25,000	25,000	34,667	37,000	42,000	42,000	3
NH	43,050	43,050	43,050	43,050	43,050	43,050	1
NJ	34,619	34,619	34,619	34,619	34,619	34,619	1
NY	39,000	39,000	42,070	42,070	45,140	45,140	2

OH	39,000	39,000	39,441	39,500	39,822	39,822	3
OK	39,060	39,060	39,530	39,530	40,000	40,000	2
PA	30,000	37,008	40,169	40,004	43,000	51,000	6
SC	34,000	34,000	34,583	34,750	35,000	35,000	3
TN	38,500	38,500	38,500	38,500	38,500	38,500	1
TX	35,000	37,000	39,757	39,021	42,500	46,000	6
UT	35,750	35,750	35,750	35,750	35,750	35,750	1
VA	40,000	47,750	48,855	49,823	52,700	54,000	5
VT	30,500	35,000	38,800	40,000	40,500	48,000	5
WA	40,000	40,000	43,073	43,073	46,145	46,145	2
WI	39,000	39,563	40,281	40,563	41,000	41,000	4

BEGINNING LIBRARIAN—CONTINUED
ALL ACADEMIC LIBRARIES

Regional Data

	Min	Q1	Mean	Median	Q3	Max	N
North Atlantic	30,000	40,000	43,179	43,000	47,647	56,000	57
Great Lakes & Plains	25,000	37,000	42,366	41,000	45,000	90,431	67
Southeast	24,710	35,000	41,878	40,000	44,000	80,776	57
West & Southwest	29,000	40,000	51,634	44,908	60,000	97,582	66
ALL REGIONS	24,710	38,000	44,917	42,000	48,958	97,582	247

State Data

	Min	Q1	Mean	Median	Q3	Max	N
AL	37,992	37,992	37,992	37,992	37,992	37,992	1
AR	37,000	37,000	38,000	38,000	39,000	39,000	2
AZ	38,000	43,000	46,912	44,908	48,723	61,932	6
CA	40,008	53,874	66,475	63,673	85,402	97,582	24
CO	35,000	36,000	40,792	39,750	42,000	52,250	6
CT	48,958	48,958	51,691	51,691	54,424	54,424	2
DC	41,000	45,600	48,692	49,000	54,000	56,000	13
FL	24,710	35,000	37,811	40,000	43,000	51,216	11
GA	30,000	39,000	47,515	42,320	51,642	77,314	13
HI	35,964	35,964	40,218	40,218	44,472	44,472	2
IA	30,282	31,200	38,811	31,200	41,795	68,923	9
ID	42,016	42,016	42,516	42,516	43,015	43,015	2
IL	33,000	41,000	43,453	43,606	46,000	57,000	15
IN	37,000	37,500	41,000	39,500	44,500	48,000	4
KS	31,413	38,579	39,986	39,537	41,000	51,000	9
KY	30,000	30,000	30,000	30,000	30,000	30,000	1
LA	30,000	30,000	36,568	32,000	40,000	50,842	5
MA	40,000	40,730	44,193	44,750	45,435	50,810	10
MD	34,800	35,700	41,417	40,500	47,000	50,000	6
ME	43,539	43,539	43,539	43,539	43,539	43,539	1
MI	36,000	40,000	45,382	43,000	49,679	60,030	9
MN	49,654	50,042	51,470	50,715	52,898	54,795	4
MO	35,875	35,875	38,125	38,500	40,000	40,000	3
MS	36,500	40,365	48,648	42,752	42,849	80,776	5

MT	30,000	30,000	36,500	36,500	43,000	43,000	2
NC	33,000	35,175	40,755	37,465	40,008	67,742	8
ND	25,000	30,500	35,000	36,500	39,500	42,000	4
NH	43,050	43,050	43,050	43,050	43,050	43,050	1
NJ	34,619	34,619	38,060	38,060	41,500	41,500	2
NM	39,428	39,428	39,428	39,428	39,428	39,428	1
NV	45,948	45,948	45,948	45,948	45,948	45,948	1
NY	30,000	33,422	38,871	39,000	45,140	46,791	5
OH	35,000	39,000	48,751	39,500	39,822	90,431	5
OK	29,000	29,000	36,020	39,060	40,000	40,000	3
PA	30,000	37,504	40,279	40,004	42,717	51,000	12
SC	34,000	34,000	34,583	34,750	35,000	35,000	3
SD	40,000	40,000	40,000	40,000	40,000	40,000	1
TN	38,500	38,500	38,500	38,500	38,500	38,500	1
TX	35,000	38,000	44,659	40,428	48,784	64,000	11
UT	35,750	35,750	41,875	41,875	48,000	48,000	2
VA	40,000	40,000	47,379	48,787	52,700	54,000	6
VT	30,500	35,000	38,800	40,000	40,500	48,000	5
WA	39,500	40,000	46,553	47,541	50,814	53,924	6
WI	39,000	39,563	40,281	40,563	41,000	41,000	4
WV	30,768	30,768	30,768	30,768	30,768	30,768	1

Discussion

Summary of Results

People interested in a particular type of library, particular type of work or a particular region will have their own way of drawing conclusions from the results of this survey. However, the results may be summarized in a very general way by noting that this survey included 16,258 individual salaries ranging from $22,000 to $331,200 with a mean of $58,960 ($57,809 in 2007, an increase of two percent) and a median of $53,521 ($53,000 in 2007, an increase of one percent). It may be useful to look at mean and median salaries paid to particular types of positions, mean and median salaries paid by particular types of libraries and mean and median salaries paid in particular geographic areas of the United States.

All of the data, since 2006, from the *ALA-APA Salary Survey: Librarian—Public and Academic* (*Librarian*) and *ALA-APA Salary Survey: Non-MLS—Public and Academic* (*Non-MLS*) are included in the *ALA-APA Library Salary Database*. Visit http://cs.ala.org/websurvey/salarysurvey/salarysurveyform/form.cfm for subscription information.

Salaries by Type of Position

The six positions are shown in Table 1 in rank order by mean of salaries paid in Public and Academic Libraries. Tables 2 and 3 compare the difference in mean salaries from 2007 to 2008 for the six positions by library category.

The 2008 sample of public libraries included all population served ranges. The opportunity for state level analysis was improved by enlarging the sample size.

Data presented in the academic salary tables for the six categories are distinguished as follows:

- Director/Dean/Chief Officer—**includes Association of Research Libraries (ARL) member data**
- Deputy/Associate/Assistant Director—**includes ARL member data**
- Department Head/Branch Manager/Coordinator/Senior Manager
- Manager/Supervisor of Support Staff
- Librarian who does not supervise—**includes ARL member data**
- Beginning Librarian—**includes ARL member data**

Table 1: Rank Order of Position Types by Mean of Salaries Paid, 2008

	ALL Regional Salary Data	N
Director/Dean/Chief Officer	89,641	973
Deputy/Associate/Assistant Director	76,574	1,152
Department Head/Branch Manager/Coordinator/Senior Manager	60,928	3,959
Manager/Supervisor of Support Staff	52,541	2,211
Librarian Who Does Not Supervise	51,370	6,858
Beginning Librarian	43,552	1,105
Total		16,258

Table 2. Rank Order of Position Types by Mean of Salaries Paid, Public Libraries, Comparison 2007 and 2008

	PUBLIC Regional Salary Data		Difference in Mean Salaries	N (2008)
	2007	2008		
Director/Dean/Chief Officer	77,200	86,354	9,154	584
Deputy/Associate/Assistant Director	74,942	73,385	-1,557	624
Department Head/Branch Manager/Coordinator/Senior Manager	60,327	60,835	508	3,508
Manager/Supervisor of Support Staff	50,722	51,594	872	1,596
Librarian Who Does Not Supervise	47,772	48,167	395	4,570
Beginning Librarian	41,334	42,601	1,267	826
Total				11,707

Data presented in the public libraries tables for the six positions are distinguished by population served as follows:

- Very Small—serving less than 10,000
- Small—serving 10,000–24,999
- Medium—serving 25,000–99,999
- Large—serving 100,000–499,999
- Very large—serving 500,000 or more

Data presented in the academic libraries tables for the six positions are distinguished by type of library as follows:

- Two-Year College
- Four-Year College
- University (including Association of Research Libraries members)

Salaries Reported

At the 2007 American Library Association Midwinter Meeting in Seattle, Washington, the ALA-APA Council voted to approve a Nonbinding Minimum Salary for Professional Librarians of $40,000 (see Appendix E). The

tables below of Highest Mean, Lowest Mean, Highest Actual and Lowest Actual illustrate the range of salaries commanded by librarians with an ALA-accredited Master's Degree (ALA MLS). The minimum salary of $40,000 was promoted as a vehicle to assist in salary improvement efforts for librarians in small, rural and poorly-funded libraries and to establish a baseline for salaries for beginning librarians. The minimum salary and the ALA-APA Better Salaries and Pay Equity Toolkit (http://www.ala-apa.org/toolkit.pdf) are tools that have been successfully used to increase salaries for librarians.

Highest Mean Salaries Reported

Directors of University (including Association of Research Libraries members), Very Large and Large public libraries earned the highest mean salaries. There were twelve mean and ten median salaries above $100,000, of which ten are shown in Table 4. In 2007, there were thirteen means above $100,000. The salaries are arrayed high to low by mean. It is worth noting that the means and medians are more than $9,000 apart in cases 4, 6, 9 and 10.

Table 3. Rank Order of Position Types by Mean of Salaries Paid, Academic Libraries, Comparison 2007 and 2008

	ACADEMIC Regional Salary Data		Difference in Mean Salaries	N (2008)
	2007	2008		
Director/Dean/Chief Officer	88,902	94,567	5,665	389
Deputy/Associate/Assistant Director	77,372	80,062	2,690	528
Department Head/Branch Manager/Coordinator/Senior Manager	65,270	61,412	-3,858	451
Librarian Who Does Not Supervise	54,959	54,684	-275	2,289
Manager/Supervisor of Support Staff	51,666	54,376	2,710	615
Beginning Librarian	48,365	44,917	-3,448	279
Total				4,551

Table 4. Highest Mean and Median Salaries Reported

Position	Region	Library Type	Mean	Median	N
Director/Dean/Chief Officer	North Atlantic	Very Large Public	172,492	167,063	6
Director/Dean/Chief Officer	West & Southwest	Very Large Public	142,434	141,276	32
Director/Dean/Chief Officer	Great Lakes & Plains	Very Large Public	135,899	133,900	5
Director/Dean/Chief Officer	Southeast	Very Large Public	134,103	124,688	12
Director/Dean/Chief Officer	West & Southwest	University	124,357	123,688	42
Director/Dean/Chief Officer	North Atlantic	University	120,643	106,000	44
Director/Dean/Chief Officer	West & Southwest	Large Public	119,068	115,282	52
Director/Dean/Chief Officer	Southeast	University	109,250	105,840	55
Director/Dean/Chief Officer	Great Lakes & Plains	University	107,654	96,469	57
Director/Dean/Chief Officer	North Atlantic	Large Public	105,841	94,635	15

Lowest Mean Salaries Reported

The lowest mean salaries reported were found across all regions and in most library types, as shown in Table 5. There were only six mean and seven median salaries below $35,000, as opposed to ten and nine in 2007. The salaries are arrayed from low to high by mean. The only positions not represented in this table are Director and Department Head.

Highest Actual Salaries Reported

There were twenty-six salaries reported above $180,000 in 2008, compared to nine in 2007 and twenty-four in 2006. Ten salaries are reported in Table 6, and there were no outlier salaries.

Lowest Actual Salaries Reported

Forty-two salaries below $22,000 were removed from the sample, in keeping with a long-standing practice of the *Librarian Salary Survey*. With these salaries excluded, there were only twelve salaries reported below $25,000, as compared to 28 in 2007. As Table 7 indicates, there was great variety in the positions, types of libraries and regions where the lowest salaries were reported, though no Directors or Department Heads are on this list.

Complicating Factors

There were several complications as a result of the change in sampling methodology briefly discussed in the Introduction and Results sections.

- Response Rate
- Position Description Changes
- Non-Responses

This salary survey also shares many of the complicating factors that will always be associated with conducting a salary survey of librarians:

- The Meaning of "Full-Time"
- The Meaning of "Professional" and "ALA-accredited master's degrees"

Several of the complications we have identified are discussed at length below.

Table 5. Lowest Mean and Median Salaries Reported

Position	Region	Library Type	Mean	Median	N
Librarian Who Does Not Supervise	West & Southwest	Very Small Public	26,363	26,363	1
Beginning Librarian	Great Lakes & Plains	Very Small Public	30,227	29,568	6
Manager/Supervisor Of Support Staff	Great Lakes & Plains	Very Small Public	31,361	31,361	2
Librarian Who Does Not Supervise	Great Lakes & Plains	Very Small Public	31,600	29,123	7
Deputy/Associate/Assistant Director	Great Lakes & Plains	Very Small Public	32,199	34,278	3
Beginning Librarian	West & Southwest	4-Year College	33,375	32,500	4
Librarian Who Does Not Supervise	Southeast	Very Small Public	35,543	34,146	3
Beginning Librarian	Southeast	2-Year College	35,922	36,718	10
Beginning Librarian	North Atlantic	Very Large Public	37,672	38,410	7
Librarian Who Does Not Supervise	North Atlantic	Very Small Public	38,098	39,256	9

Table 6. Highest Actual Salaries Reported

Position	Region	Library Type	Maximum Salary Reported
Director/Dean/Chief Officer	Great Lakes & Plains	University	331,200
Director/Dean/Chief Officer	North Atlantic	University	281,400
Director/Dean/Chief Officer	North Atlantic	University	246,000
Director/Dean/Chief Officer	Southeast	University	240,000
Director/Dean/Chief Officer	Great Lakes & Plains	University	239,500
Director/Dean/Chief Officer	North Atlantic	University	235,380
Director/Dean/Chief Officer	Southeast	University	222,585
Director/Dean/Chief Officer	North Atlantic	Very Large Public	220,000
Director/Dean/Chief Officer	North Atlantic	Very Large Public	220,000
Director/Dean/Chief Officer	Great Lakes & Plains	University	220,000

Response Rate

The sample of libraries invited to participate in the survey was 3,484. Since 2006, the sample has been almost three times as large as prior years to capture and report region- and state-level data. We continue our efforts to supply the library community with more comprehensive national- and state-level salary data for managers developing budgets and salary ranges and to assist job seekers. Despite the size of the sample, the overall response rates for regions and states were too low to be statistically significant. However, we have included all of the data at both levels and encourage all readers to be conscious of the number of responses when using the data. We anticipate higher response levels in the future.

To increase the response rate, the deadline for the survey was extended by two weeks from March 14 to March 23, with reminder postcards sent to non-respondents.

It is worth noting that the number of responding libraries has been rather consistent, with the exception of 2005 (see Table 8). This was the first year the sample was increased to include state-level analysis. Respondents seems to be comfortable with the web-based survey, with larger institutions given the opportunity to provide data by fax or emailed spreadsheets. Uncovering the reason for the response reduction is difficult because there are many factors involved. It may be the change in timing since many surveys are conducted in the early part of the year (see Figure 1). Perhaps a later survey is preferable. The contact information may have been more accurate in 2005, thus leading to more libraries receiving and responding. Or it may have simply been a matter of libraries being more willing to participate in a survey issued by ALA rather than ALA-APA, a lesser known entity.

A selection of the 123 members of the Association of Research Libraries (ARL) was

Table 7. Lowest Actual Salaries Reported

Position	Region	Library Type	Minimum Salary Reported
Librarian Who Does Not Supervise	Southeast	Medium Public	22,000
Librarian Who Does Not Supervise	Southeast	Very Large Public	22,089
Beginning Librarian	North Atlantic	Very Small Public	22,650
Librarian Who Does Not Supervise	North Atlantic	Small Public	22,880
Manager/Supervisor Of Support Staff	North Atlantic	Small Public	22,880
Deputy/Associate/Assistant Director	Southeast	University	23,067
Librarian Who Does Not Supervise	Great Lakes & Plains	Large Public	23,478
Librarian Who Does Not Supervise	Southeast	Medium Public	23,712
Beginning Librarian	Great Lakes & Plains	Very Small Public	23,858
Librarian Who Does Not Supervise	North Atlantic	Very Small Public	24,224
Beginning Librarian	Southeast	2-Year College	24,710
Beginning Librarian	Great Lakes & Plains	Medium Public	24,988

Table 8. Salary Survey Response Rates, 2000–2008

Year and Survey	Sample	Responses	Response Rate (%)
2008—Librarian	3,484	1,010	29
2007—Librarian and Non-MLS combined	3,484	834	24
2006—Librarian	3,418	1,053	31
2006—Non-MLS	3,418	836	24
2005—Librarian	4,343	2,058	47
2004—Librarian	1,275	881	69
2003—Librarian	1,268	901	72
2002—Librarian	1,320	924	70
2001—Librarian	1,297	866	67
2000—Librarian	1,294	931	72

asked for permission to use the salary data they had already provided to ARL. Of the 71 that were invited, 36 (51 percent) granted permission to use their data for the four positions listed above as "includes Association of Research Libraries member data (ARL)." The response from ARL members was eight points higher this year.

To alleviate confusion for respondents, the survey Web page listed ARL members and led those members to a specific web page. ARL members were also sent a different letter, requesting permission (see Appendix C).

Position Description Changes

This survey includes the six positions that have been used and honed over many years. For every salary survey, there are exceptions to the positions we have chosen to include. As library hierarchies and management styles have changed, it has become challenging to assign incumbents to one position. We appreciate respondents' willingness to find the best fit.

The questionnaire instructions stated, "If the responsibilities of a job in the survey align with positions in your library, report data for the matched position. If jobs do not coincide with the majority of duties to those in the survey, or the position is not full-time, do not report data for that job." We recognize that libraries are organized differently.

One position title was changed slightly from 2007: Librarians Who Do Not Supervise was altered to be Librarian Who Does Not Supervise.

Non-Responses

In total, 71 percent of libraries sampled did not respond to the survey. We will be conducting follow-up research to assess how to increase the response rate to previous levels, although the rate is satisfactory for a national survey and regional data is typically statistically significant.

The Meaning of "Full-Time"

The questionnaire asked about salaries for full-time and part-time incumbents. Smaller libraries depend on part-time staff at all levels, and it is not unusual for staff in librarian positions to be part-time. If no hours were designated, 40 hours was assumed. All salaries were converted to full-time salaries, based on a 40-hour work week, for the purposes of analysis.

The months in a year problem affects academic and public libraries where librarians sometimes have contracts for less than twelve months or the number of hours considered to be full-time may be anywhere between 30 and 40 hours. In the survey, all salaries are treated as full-time salaries, regardless of the number of months or hours actually worked.

The Meaning of "Professional" and "ALA-Accredited Master's Degrees"

Who is a librarian? This is not a simple question. In smaller, rural and branch public libraries, the director may not have a Master's degree in Library and/or Information Science and/or Studies. ALA policy 54.2 Librarians: Appropriate Degrees states, "The master's degree from a program accredited by the American Library Association (or from a master's level program in library and information studies accredited or recognized by the appropriate national body of another country) is the appropriate professional degree for librarians." For this survey, we asked respondents in libraries with three or more staff members to report only staff with master's degrees from programs in library and information studies (MLS) accredited by American Library Association (ALA). In past surveys, we have asked the respondent to make a decision based on the definition in ALA's statement on "Library and Information Studies Education and Human Resource Utilization"—(http://www.ala.org/ala/hrdr/educprofdev/lepu.pdf).

Figure 1. Salary Survey Methodology Changes, 2005 and 2008

	2005	2008
Conducted by	Library Research Center, University of Illinois at Urbana Champaign	Management Association of Illinois
Survey Period	May–June, extended to July	January–March
Salaries as of	April 1	February 1
Return Address on Envelope	American Library Association	ALA-APA

Appendix A. Survey Questionnaire and Cover Letters

2008 LIBRARIAN SALARY SURVEY

PLEASE PRINT

UserID: *(listed on cover letter)*: _____

Name of Library _____

Questionnaire completed by _____

Phone (include area code) _____ Ext. _____

E-Mail Address _____

⟹ **COMPLETED SURVEY DUE FEBRUARY 29, 2008**

BENEFITS

Please indicate (✓) below what benefits your library provides and which staff are eligible. Use your own definitions of full-time and part-time. Do not report benefits that are for the director only as determined by contract negotiations.

Benefit:	Full-time Professional Staff	Part-time Professional Staff	Full-time Support Staff	Part-time Support Staff
a. Bereavement leave	☐	☐	☐	☐
b. Child care	☐	☐	☐	☐
c. Credit union	☐	☐	☐	☐
d. Dental insurance	☐	☐	☐	☐
e. Disability insurance	☐	☐	☐	☐
f. Elder care	☐	☐	☐	☐
g. Flexible spending plans	☐	☐	☐	☐
h. Health insurance	☐	☐	☐	☐
i. Life insurance	☐	☐	☐	☐
j. Long-term care	☐	☐	☐	☐
k. Pension	☐	☐	☐	☐
l. Personal days	☐	☐	☐	☐
m. Prescription benefits	☐	☐	☐	☐
n. Professional memberships	☐	☐	☐	☐
o. Retirement savings	☐	☐	☐	☐
p. Sick leave	☐	☐	☐	☐
q. Training & education	☐	☐	☐	☐
r. Transportation subsidies	☐	☐	☐	☐
s. Tuition reimbursement	☐	☐	☐	☐
t. Vacation	☐	☐	☐	☐
u. Vision insurance	☐	☐	☐	☐
v. Other (please describe)				

LIBRARY NAME: _____

USERID: _____

PHONE: _____

ALA·APA
Allied Professional Association
the Organization for the Advancement of Library Employees

2008 LIBRARIAN SALARY SURVEY
PAY DATA SHEET

ALA
American Library Association

Due: February 29, 2008		
When reporting multiple incumbents in the same Job Code, "Job Title" need only be entered once *if* it is the same for all incumbents.		
JOB CODE (use from survey)	JOB TITLE (use from survey)	ACTUAL BASE SALARY (no averages)	# OF EMPLOYEES AT RATE

COPY THIS PAGE FIRST IF YOU HAVE MORE DATA THAN WILL FIT IN THE ROWS PROVIDED.

2008 LIBRARIAN SALARY SURVEY

1. PARTICIPATION OPTIONS:
(available at http://www.hrsource.org/images/mail/ala.html):

a) **Online**. See the cover letter for your userID/password and then login here: http://64.62.165.7/olstart/olsite/. This is our preferred method of receiving your information.

b) **Spreadsheet**. Download the custom MS Excel spreadsheet and e-mail it back to Jean Hannon: jhannon@hrsource.org.

c) **Paper**. Use this questionnaire to record your information using the job descriptions to match your jobs. Then fax or mail <u>the first page</u> and the <u>pay data sheet</u> to:

> The Management Association of Illinois
> Attn: Compensation Department
> 1400 Opus Place, Suite 500
> Downers Grove, IL 60515
> 630-963-2800 FAX

2. BEFORE STARTING, PLEASE READ THE **INSTRUCTIONS** AND **JOB DESCRIPTIONS**

3. FILL OUT AND RETURN ONLY THE **COVER PAGE** AND **PAY DATA SHEET**

4. THANK YOU FOR PARTICIPATING!

2008 LIBRARIAN SALARY SURVEY
INSTRUCTIONS

MATCHING JOBS

This survey requests annual salaries paid to full-time professional librarians, i.e., persons who have master's degrees from library and information studies programs accredited by the ALA. It is our expectation that each full-time professional librarian on your library's staff will fit into one of the six categories in this survey. Therefore, salaries for all full-time professional librarians should be reported while salaries for part-time professional librarians should **NOT** be reported.

Read the position descriptions carefully and compare them to jobs in your organization. If the responsibilities of a job in the survey align with the majority of duties of your position, report data for the matched position. If jobs do not coincide with the majority of the duties to those in the survey, or the position is not full-time, do not report data for that job.

REPORTING PAY

Use the following **2008 Librarian Salary Survey Pay Data Sheet** to provide us with data for each staff member who occupies a position in your organization that matches at least 50% to our job descriptions. Each row in the spreadsheet should represent one incumbent at your organization as we do not want averages, we want actual pay data. Report salaries paid by the library budget which are filled closest to February 1, 2008.

Do not:
- Report data for vacant positions
- Split salaries between job codes
- Report the same incumbent in more than one position
- Report data for graduate students who are working as part of an assistantship
- Provide data for a position with less than a 50% match to the job description
- Include benefits

JOB CODE
Please provide the job code from the survey job descriptions for which you are reporting data.

JOB TITLE
Please provide the job title from the survey job descriptions for which you are reporting data.

ACTUAL BASE SALARY
Salaries are defined as actual **straight time** pay. Do not provide averages. Do not include benefits, overtime premiums, shift differentials, bonuses, or any other incentives or variable pay components.

2008 LIBRARIAN SALARY SURVEY
INSTRUCTIONS – *continued*

NUMBER OF EMPLOYEES AT RATE

If your library has more than one incumbent for a position and they are being paid different annual salaries, please enter each annual salary separately and indicate the number of employees at each rate.

For example:

JOB CODE (Use from survey)	JOB TITLE	ACTUAL ANNUAL BASE SALARY: (No averages)	# OF EMPLOYEES AT RATE
1	Beginning Librarian	23000	1
1	Beginning Librarian	25000	2
6	Librarian	35000	3
6	Librarian	40000	2

SPECIAL NOTES FOR ACADEMIC LIBRARIES

Salaries for staff working less than 12 months in a year should be reported as the actual salary without making adjustments for the reduced work year.

If services are contributed (i.e., the institution pays some expenses or an honorarium but not a true salary), please do not list the incumbent.

QUESTIONS?

If you have any questions or problems completing this questionnaire, please contact Jean Hannon at (800) 448-4584 ext. 238 jhannon@hrsource.org, Monica Zborowski ext 265 mzborowski@hrsource.org or Kristy Williams ext 252 kwilliams@hrsource.org.

FOR YOUR RECORDS: KEEP A COPY OF ALL REPORTED DATA

2008 LIBRARIAN SALARY SURVEY

1. Beginning Librarian
List annual salaries of staff hired in the last six months for full-time work with a master's degrees from programs in library and information studies accredited by the ALA, but no professional experience after receiving the degree.

2. Director / Dean / Chief Officer
List the annual salary of the chief officer of the library or library system. Report only full-time staff with master's degrees from programs in library and information studies accredited by the ALA. Do not repeat salaries reported for position 1.

3. Deputy / Associate / Assistant Director
List annual salaries of employees who report to the Director and manage major aspects of the library operation (e.g., technical services, public services, collection development, systems/automation). Report only full-time staff with master's degrees from programs in library and information studies accredited by the ALA. Do not repeat salaries reported for position 1.

4. Department Head / Branch Manager / Coordinator / Senior Manager
List annual salaries of full-time employees who supervise one or more professional librarians. Report only full-time staff with master's degrees from programs in library and information studies accredited by the ALA. Do not repeat salaries reported for position 1.

5. Manager / Supervisor of Support Staff
List annual salaries of full-time employees who supervise support staff in any part of the library but do *not* supervise professional librarians. Report only full-time staff with master's degrees from programs in library and information studies accredited by the ALA. Do not repeat salaries reported for position 1.

6. Librarians Who Do Not Supervise
List annual salaries of full-time staff who were not reported earlier and who do not have supervisory responsibilities. Report only full-time staff with master's degrees from programs in library and information studies accredited by the ALA. Do not repeat salaries reported for position 1.

January 17, 2008

Dear Colleague:

You are invited to participate in the annual *ALA-APA Library Salary Survey—Librarians: Public and Academic*. **For 2008, we are only collecting salary data for six librarian titles.** Your library is one of a scientifically selected sample and your response is critical. For those of you who are unfamiliar with the *Librarian Salary Survey*, it provides the library community with sound salary data by state, region, library size, and type. Please help us reach the necessary 50% response rate. **The deadline is February 29, 2008.**

All responding institutions receive the benefit of 25% off the print price of the *Librarian Salary Survey*. **In addition, this year we will give responding institutions 30 days of FREE access to the *Library Salary Database*,** which includes librarian and non-MLS salaries from 2006 to the present. The ALA-APA *Library Salary Database*—http://cs.ala.org/websurvey/salarysurvey/login/login.cfm—allows users to run reports on more than 65 library positions in academic and public libraries by library type, state and region.

The survey is being conducted *online* with the assistance of The Management Association of Illinois. Your library has a unique identifier to access the survey (noted at the top of this letter). You may choose among several methods to complete the survey. The instructions and Web address are on the enclosed instruction page. Libraries that participated via Excel spreadsheet last year may receive a copy of their 2007 spreadsheet file upon request.

We want this to be a successful survey and will work with you to ensure your library's response. If you have any questions, problems, or technical difficulties, please contact The Management Association of Illinois' Survey Department at 800-448-4584.

The ALA-Allied Professional Association continues to work in consultation with the American Library Association Office for Research and Statistics to provide salary data. In 2009, we will again collect both librarian and non-MLS salary data. For free access to the database, complete the contact information at the end of the survey. For the 25% discount on the price of the report, mention your participation when you place your order with the ALA Store—http://www.alastore.ala.org or 866-746-7252. The Survey will be available in print in the summer of 2008. Call 800-545-2433, x2424 for more information.

Sincerely yours,

Keith Michael Fiels
Executive Director, American Library Association-Allied Professional Association

For Online Participation:
LIBRARY DIRECTOR OR HR DIRECTOR
UserID:
Password: (case sensitive)

Dear Library Director/Dean:

It's time again to help our profession gather accurate, timely and comprehensive salary data. We are asking permission from Association of Research Libraries (ARL) members to use salary data for positions that ARL collects which are similar to those in the ALA-APA survey. We will, of course, treat this data confidentially. It is very important that we include your data in our annual survey of librarian salaries.

The deadline for giving us your permission is February 29, 2008. Please complete either the enclosed questionnaire or the *online* permission form: http://64.62.165.7/olstart/olsite/. Your library has a unique identifier to access the survey (noted at the top of this letter). *We would also appreciate it if you would answer the supplemental questions on our survey about benefits provided to staff.*

As our thank you, this year we will give responding institutions 30 days of FREE access to the *Library Salary Database*, which includes librarian and non-MLS salaries from 2006 to the present. The ALA-APA *Library Salary Database*—http://cs.ala.org/websurvey/salarysurvey/login/login.cfm—allows users to run reports on more than 65 library positions by library type, state and region.

If you have any questions, problems, or technical difficulties, please contact The Management Association of Illinois' Survey Department at 800-448-4584.

For free access to the database, please complete the contact information on the website. Your library is also entitled to a 25% discount on the price of the report when you place your order with the ALA Store http://www.alastore.ala.org or 866-746-7252. The Survey will be available in print in summer 2008. Call 800-545-2433, x2424 for more information.

FYI—in 2009 we will again collect salary data on non-MLS positions in libraries.

Sincerely yours,

Keith Michael Fiels
Executive Director, American Library Association-Allied Professional Association

Appendix B. Methodology

Formation of Library Groups

As in previous years, the survey samples were selected from two library universes—public and academic. The public library universe included all public libraries and was stratified into five classes using the 2005 public library file: Very Small, serving populations less than 10,000; Small, serving 10,000–24,999; Medium, serving 25,000–99,999; Large, serving 100,000–499,999; and Very Large, serving 500,000 or more.

The academic library universe was stratified into three categories: Two-Year college, Four-Year college and University (including Association of Research Libraries members' data) using the 2006 Academic Library Survey file (the most current and complete file available). This file includes codes for the categories created by the Carnegie Foundation for the Advancement of Teaching in 1994. Our "Two-Year college" corresponds to the Carnegie category "Associate of Arts." Our "Four-Year college" category corresponds to the Carnegie Categories "Baccalaureate I and II." Our "University" includes the Carnegie categories "Master's I and II, Doctoral I and II, and Research I and II."

Sample Selection and Return

The sample frame for each type/size/geographic strata was determined by using a proportional sampling procedure that took into account the size of the population in each group (unduplicated population served or student full-time enrollment) and a 95 percent confidence interval, ±5 percent. The public library sample was selected using the *Public Libraries in the United States: Fiscal Year 2005* data reported by state library agencies as part of the National Center for Education Statistics (NCES) Federal State Cooperative System for Public Library Data (FSCS). The file includes data on all ALA-accredited and non-ALA-accredited MLS and other staff. After selecting the sample, The Management Association of Illinois dropped from the sampling frame libraries that had refused to respond to previous salary surveys. One thousand nine hundred and eighty-eight (1,988) public libraries were surveyed.

The procedure for selecting the academic library sample was similar to the procedure followed in previous years for the *Survey of Librarian Salaries*. The ALA created a sampling frame using the 2006 National Center for Education Statistics (NCES) data files *Academic Libraries: 2006* and *Public Libraries in the United States: Fiscal Year 2005*, excluding libraries with two or fewer staff and using a 95% confidence interval, ±5 percent.[1] This file includes data on the number of staff who hold ALA-accredited MLS degrees and "librarians and other professionals." Also removed were institutions that had closed (3), and two (2) that could not be confirmed from either the 2005 or 2006 NCES data files. Then ALA's Office for Research and Statistics screened out several sets of institutions categorized as "specialized" by the Carnegie Corporation for the Advancement of Teaching. Those institutions offer degrees ranging from the bachelor's to the doctorate, at least 50 percent of which are in a single specialized field, e.g., "theological seminaries, Bible colleges and other institutions offering degrees in religion," and "Schools of art, music and design." Specialized institutions often declined to respond in the early years of this survey. Also excluded were four sets of institutions whose individual members had been unable to respond in the past. In New York, the seventeen institutions that are part of the City University of New York were removed because librarians there have full academic status and salary is not related to position description. Public Two-Year colleges in California were removed for the same reason, as were the fourteen members of the state university system in Pennsylvania. Also in Pennsylvania, ALA removed all but the main campus of Pennsylvania State University because librarians at other campuses declined to respond in the past and referred us to the main campus. One thousand, four hundred ninety-six (1,496) academic libraries were surveyed.

A total of 3,484 surveys were sent and a total of 1,010 responses were analyzed for this report.

Procedure

The cover letter was mailed in January 2008 to academic and public libraries with directions

---

1. The academic libraries sample was drawn from the 2006 post-survey file provided by the U.S. Census Bureau solely for the purposes of this study.

for participating online, participating using MS Excel spreadsheets or downloading and printing a paper survey. A separate letter was sent to ARL members asking for permission to use their data.

Respondents could complete the survey in several ways: through a secure website, on an MS Excel spreadsheet that could be faxed or emailed to The Management Association of Illinois (The Association), by emailing or faxing a report generated by a Human Resources enterprise application or software to The Association or by calling The Association with the information. The Association for Research Libraries (ARL) and all but the largest public libraries (serving 500,000 or more) completed the survey electronically via the established website.

A reminder postcard was sent to all non-respondents in March, reminding them of the deadline of March 14. The deadline was extended and the web survey closed on March 23, and all responses were cleaned and analyzed using SPSS for Windows.

ARL Libraries
ARL Libraries were asked for permission to use the ARL data for positions that closely match ALA-APA ALA MLS survey positions. The codes used were DIRLIB, ASCDIR, ASTDIR, PUBS, TECH, ADMIN, REF and CAT.

Large and Very Large Public Libraries
Large and Very Large public libraries were mailed a copy of the questionnaire, but also were given the option of participating online, using MS Excel spreadsheets or returning their paper survey to The Association. Data from paper surveys received at The Association were entered online by Association staff.

Table B-1. States in Four Regions of the U.S.

North Atlantic	Great Lakes & Plains	Southeast	West & Southwest
Connecticut	Illinois	Alabama	Alaska
Delaware	Indiana	Arkansas	Arizona
District of Columbia	Iowa	Florida	California
Maine	Kansas	Georgia	Colorado
Maryland	Michigan	Kentucky	Hawaii
Massachusetts	Minnesota	Louisiana	Idaho
New Hampshire	Missouri	Mississippi	Montana
New Jersey	Nebraska	North Carolina	Nevada
New York	North Dakota	South Carolina	New Mexico
Pennsylvania	Ohio	Tennessee	Oklahoma
Rhode Island	South Dakota	Virginia	Oregon
Vermont	Wisconsin	West Virginia	Texas
			Utah
			Washington
			Wyoming

Source: *Statistics of Public Libraries, 1977–1978* (NCES, 1982)

Table B-2. Very Large Public Libraries: Size of Sample, Return

	Sample	Return	
	#	#	% of Sample
North Atlantic	12	8	66.67
Great Lakes & Plains	10	5	50.00
Southeast	20	12	60.00
West & Southwest	40	33	82.50
TOTAL	82	58	70.73

Table B-3. Large Public Libraries: Size of Sample, Return

	Sample	Return	
	#	#	% of Sample
North Atlantic	35	15	42.86
Great Lakes & Plains	76	47	61.84
Southeast	114	49	42.98
West & Southwest	112	55	49.11
TOTAL	337	166	49.26

Table B-4. Medium-Sized Public Libraries: Size of Sample, Return

	Sample	Return	
	#	#	% of Sample
North Atlantic	151	37	24.50
Great Lakes & Plains	138	64	46.38
Southeast	119	24	20.17
West & Southwest	97	40	41.24
TOTAL	505	165	32.67

Table B-5. Small Public Libraries: Size of Sample, Return

	Sample	Return	
	#	#	% of Sample
North Atlantic	193	49	25.39
Great Lakes & Plains	205	60	29.27
Southeast	64	11	17.19
West & Southwest	61	12	19.67
TOTAL	523	132	25.24

Table B-6. Very Small Public Libraries: Size of Sample, Return

	Sample	Return	
	#	#	% of Sample
North Atlantic	176	37	21.02
Great Lakes & Plains	285	39	13.68
Southeast	21	5	23.81
West & Southwest	59	7	11.86
TOTAL	541	88	16.27

Table B-7. Two-Year College Libraries: Size of Sample, Return

	Sample	Return	
	#	#	% of Sample
North Atlantic	116	14	12.07
Great Lakes & Plains	91	12	13.19
Southeast	135	17	12.59
West & Southwest	197	50	25.38
TOTAL	529	93	17.25

Table B-8. Four-Year College Libraries: Size of Sample, Return

	Sample	Return	
	#	#	% of Sample
North Atlantic	111	31	27.93
Great Lakes & Plains	111	35	31.53
Southeast	109	26	23.85
West & Southwest	42	17	40.48
TOTAL	373	109	29.22

Table B-9. University and ARL Libraries: Size of Sample, Return

	Sample	Return	
	#	#	% of Sample
North Atlantic	169	44	26.03
Great Lakes & Plains	146	55	37.67
Southeast	131	56	44.75
West & Southwest	138	44	31.88
TOTAL	584	199	34.08

Table B-10. All Libraries Surveyed: Size of Sample, Return

	Sample	Return	
	#	#	% of Sample
	Sent	Returned	Response Rate
North Atlantic	963	235	24.40
Great Lakes & Plains	1062	317	29.85
Southeast	713	200	28.05
West & Southwest	746	258	34.58
TOTAL	3484	1010	28.99

Appendix C. Compensation Surveys Providing Information on Library Workers

Most library salary surveys listed below are conducted on a regular schedule (annual or biennial) and on a regional or national basis. The library literature should be monitored for reports of one-time surveys by individual libraries or associations. Many state library agencies collect salary and benefits data as part of their ongoing statistical gathering efforts from libraries within their own state. There is wide variation, however, in what data are collected and how these are compiled and reported. Most collect only public library data. Academic and school library data may be collected by other state agencies.

In addition, some state and regional library associations collect salary data, issue recommended salary guidelines, set minimum salaries for professional positions or publish reports in association journals or newsletters. As of June 2008, fourteen states had established recommended minimum salaries for public library positions. These include: Connecticut, Illinois, Indiana, Iowa, Louisiana, Maine, Massachusetts, New Jersey, North Carolina, Pennsylvania, Rhode Island, Texas, Vermont and Wisconsin. Specific dollar amounts are updated regularly by the associations. The latest figures can be found periodically in the classified section of *American Libraries* or *College & Research Libraries News*. These figures are also posted on the ALA-APA website at http://www.ala-apa.org/salaries/minimumsalaries.html.

A list of state library agency addresses can be found in *The Bowker Annual: Library and Book Trade Almanac* or on the Internet at http://www.cosla.org under "Member Profiles." Library associations and ALA Chapters can be found in *The Bowker Annual: Library and Book Trade Almanac* or on the Internet at http://www.ala.org under "Our Association" then "Chapters" and "Other Groups and Organizations."

Individual libraries will sometimes conduct private surveys of institutions of comparable size or in the same geographical area, either through an outside consulting firm or by calling libraries informally. For the most part, these surveys are not published, although the initiating library will often share results with participating libraries. Some library workers are also conducting surveys that compare their salaries with other industries, professions and occupations within their jurisdiction in an effort to achieve pay equity with positions requiring comparable skills, effort, responsibilities and working conditions.

The American Library Association Policies related to salary issues may be found in the *ALA Handbook of Organization* at http://www.ala.org/ala/ourassociation/governingdocs/policymanual/librarypersonnel.htm.

Academic Libraries

Association of Research Libraries. *ARL Annual Salary Survey*. Washington, D.C.: ARL, 1973–. Updated annually.

The ARL Annual Salary Survey annually reports salaries for more than 12,000 professional positions in ARL member libraries. These data are used to determine whether salaries are competitive, equitable across institutions and personal characteristics and keeping up with inflation. The survey also tracks minority representation in ARL US libraries and reports separate data for health sciences and law libraries. Statistics have been collected and published annually since 1980. Information on this survey can be found at http://www.arl.org/stats/annualsurveys/salary.

Most current ARL publications will be available in their entirety on the ARL Web site and many are also available in print form. To order, use the online form at http://www.arl.org/resources/pubs/pubsorderform.shtml or contact the ARL Publications Distribution Center, PO Box 531, Annapolis Junction, MD 20701-0531, 301-362-8196, (fax) 301-206-9789, pubs@arl.org. The journal costs $75 for ARL Members, $145 for nonmembers.

College and University Professional Association for Human Resources. *Administrative Compensation Survey (AdComp)*. Knoxville, TN: CUPA-HR. Updated annually.

The survey provides salary and demographic data for senior-level administrative positions. There is also a short Pay Practices section asking about who the CHRO reports to and about "incentive" compensation for selected positions.

For the print edition the cost ranges from $160 to $320; for Data on Demand (online access), from $500 to $1000. Contact CUPA-HR, Tyson Place, 2607 Kingston Pike, Suite 250, Knoxville, TN 37919, 865-637-7673, (fax) 865-637-7674, http://www.cupahr.org/surveys/files/salary0708/SalSrvy08%20Order%20Form_4.30.08.doc.

College and University Professional Association for Human Resources. *Mid-Level Administrative and Professional Salary Survey (Mid-Level)*. Knoxville, TN: CUPA-HR. Updated annually.

This survey features provides salary and rate structure data for mid-level positions; survey also provides data on pay practices. See contact information above.

Public Libraries

American Library Association. Public Library Association. *Public Library Data Service Statistical Report*. Chicago, IL: PLA. Updated annually.

Published annually, the PLDS report presents exclusive, timely data from more than 800 public libraries across the United States and Canada on finances, library resources, annual use figures and technology. In addition to these valuable topics, each year's edition contains a special survey highlighting statistics on one service area or topic. To order the print version ($120 with discounts for ALA and PLA members), use the online form at http://www.ala.org/ala/pla/plapubs/pldsstatreport/PLDS2008printversion.pdf. To order the PLDS database ($250) use the online form at http://www.ala.org/ala/pla/plapubs/pldsstatreport/PLDS2008databaseform.pdf. For more information about the PLDS Statistical Report contact the PLA office at 800-545-2433, ext. 5PLA or pla@ala.org.

Evelina R. Moulder. "Salaries of Municipal Officials" in *The Municipal Year Book*. Washington, D.C.: International City/County Management Association. Updated annually.

The Municipal Year Book offers salary survey data for municipal and county officials by population group, geographic region, form of government and metro status. *The Municipal Year Book* is published in April of each year

and includes salary data from the previous year. To order, call 800-745-8780 or purchase online at http://bookstore.icma.org. The *Municipal Year Book* costs $99.

Sandstedt, Carl R. *Salary Survey: West-North-Central States*. St. Peters, Mo.: St. Charles City-County Library. Updated annually.

This annual survey provides data for directors, assistant directors, department heads, starting MLS and several support positions for public libraries in West-North-Central States (North Dakota, South Dakota, Nebraska, Kansas, Minnesota, Iowa, Missouri). Average salaries are presented by size of library budget. Also includes per FTE costs, per capita support and per capita materials budget.

St. Charles City-County Library District, 425 Spencer Rd., Box 529, St. Peters, MO 63376. Available for free online at http://www.win.org/library/library_office/reports/index.html.

School Libraries

Educational Research Service. *National Survey of Salaries and Wages in Public Schools*. Arlington, VA: ERS. Updated annually.

ERS publishes an annual report of salaries for public school personnel, which includes data for school librarians and library clerks. The report covers scheduled salaries for professional personnel and actual salaries paid for professional and support personnel by enrollment group, per pupil expenditure and geographic region. It also includes year-to-year, five-year and ten-year information on trends in public school salaries and wages, with comparisons to the Consumer Price Index for each of these periods. Available from ERS, 2000 Clarendon Blvd., Arlington, VA 22201, 800-791-9308, (fax) 703-243-1985, http://www.ers.org/surveyresearch/index.html. The price $150.

Marilyn L. Shontz, et. al. "The SLJ Spending Survey." *School Library Journal*, New York, NY. Updated periodically.

The survey includes data and tables about library media specialists' years of experience and salaries. *School Library Journal*, 360 Park Avenue South, New York, NY 10010,

646-746-6759, (fax) 646-746-6689, slj@reed-business.com, www.schoollibraryjournal.com.

Specialized Libraries

American Association of Law Libraries. *Biennial Salary Survey and Organizational Characteristics*. Chicago, IL: AALL. Updated biennially.

The report summarizes salary information for law libraries with three sections that cover academic libraries, private firm/corporate libraries and state, court and county libraries. The data is broken out and crossed-tabbed by position, region, gender, education, years in current position and years of library experience and membership in AALL.

Contact AALL, 53 W. Jackson Blvd., Suite 940, Chicago, IL 60604, 312-939-4764 x12, (fax) 312-431-1097, http://www.aallnet.org/products/pub_salary_survey.asp. AALL members may browse the online edition free of charge. The hardcopy is $110 for AALL members, $150 for non-members.

Association of Academic Health Sciences Libraries. *Annual Statistics of Medical School Libraries in the United States and Canada*. Seattle, WA: AAHSLD. Updated annually.

Salaries are provided for director, deputy director, associate director, division head, department head, other librarians and entry-level positions. Besides salary data, the survey asks the respondent for years of experience, gender, FTE supervised, ethnicity and race for each professional library staff member. Minimum, maximum and mean are provided for the positions and arranged by region.

It's available at no cost to members of AAHSL and $250 for nonmembers. To acquire the Annual Statistics, contact AAHSL, c/o Executive Director Shirley Bishop, 2150 N. 107th Street, Suite 205, Seattle, Washington 98133, (206) 367-8704, FAX (206) 367-8777; e-mail: aahsl@shirleybishopinc.com.

Medical Library Association. *Hay Group/MLA 2005 Salary Survey*. Chicago: MLA. Updated triennially.

More than 600 members provided data for the 2005 salary survey, available in summary format to MLA's members via the Association's website, http://www.mlanet.org. The summary offers detailed information by job title, geographical area, type of institution and more. Print and PDF versions are available from the MLANet store, http://www.mlanet.org/order/index.html. The print edition is $50 for members, $85 for nonmembers. The online edition is $40 for members, $75 for nonmembers. For more information, contact MLA, 65 E. Wacker Pl., Suite 1900, Chicago, IL 60601-7298, 312-419-9094.

Special Libraries Association. *SLA Annual Salary Survey*. Alexandria, VA: SLA. Updated annually.

Salaries are reported at the 10th, 25th, 50th (median), 75th and 90th percentiles and contain breakdowns by industry, geographic region, administrative responsibility, sex, education level and experience. Data for the U.S. and Canada are presented in separate tables.

The salary survey is a comprehensive report containing the most accurate U.S. and Canadian salary information gathered by a member survey. A wide variety of variables are covered including industry type, geographical area, job title, budget range and years of experience.

The report is available to SLA members for $55, $125 non-members as a PDF download or a print version. Contact Special Libraries Association, 331 S. Patrick St., Alexandria, VA 22314, 703-647-4900, http://www.sla.org/content/resources/research/salarysurveys/salsur2006/index.cfm.

More Salary Surveys for Other Library Workers and Related Information Professionals

For salary data on other types of workers that may be employed in libraries, the following surveys might be useful:

Abbott, Langer and Associates, Inc., conducts annual or biennial salary surveys for the following fields: legal and related jobs in business and industry; industrial engineers; plant and facilities managers and engineers; consulting engineering firms; consulting firms; independent lab/testing/inspection firms; geologists; human resources/personnel department; service department;

nonprofit organizations; research and development: manufacturing; food and beverage processing; security/loss prevention dept.; MIS/data processing; accounting departments; accounting firms; advertising agencies; sales/marketing management; direct marketing; life sciences and telecommunications.

All Nonprofit Organizations. Updated annually.

This report provides pay data on benchmark jobs in nonprofit organizations (including a Director of Information). It reports by type of organization, number of employees, fiscal size, geographic scope of service and location; it also compares each type of organization to each other variable. Part 1 is $344.50; Part 2 is $689.00.

For more information, contact Abbott, Langer and Associates at 548 First St., Crete, IL 60417, 708-672-4200, (fax) 708-672-4674, http://www.abbott-langer.com.

Grady, Jenifer and Denise Davis. *ALA-APA Salary Survey: Non-MLS—Public and Academic.* Chicago: American Library Association-Allied Professional Association. Updated annually.

This survey is a gathering of information on discrete positions within the library that do not require a MLS degree from an ALA-accredited institution. The information is reported for both public and academic libraries. The two library universes are stratified by regions and states for analysis. This publication is $100, $90 to ALA members and is available from the ALA Online Store, 866-746-7252, http://www.alastore.ala.org. For more information about the Non-MLS Salary Survey, contact ALA-APA at info@ala-apa.org or call 800-545-2433 x2424.

Library Mosaics was a bi-monthly magazine for support staff in libraries, media and information centers. The last support staff salary survey published by *Library Mosaics* was the "2003 Salary Survey" by Raymond Roney and Charlie Fox in the July/August issue. The magazine collected and reported six support staff salary surveys between 1989 and 2003. It provides a general overview of support staff salaries, salary ceilings and pay equity. For past issues, contact *Library Mosaics*, Yenor,

Inc., PO Box 5171, Culver City, CA 90231, 310-645-4998.

U.S. Department of Labor, Bureau of Labor Statistics, National Compensation Survey program annually produces information on wages by occupation for many metropolitan areas and also for the nation as a whole. It provides data on occupational earnings, employer costs for wages, salaries, benefits and details of employer-provided benefit and establishment practices. This umbrella program combines the Occupational Compensation Surveys, the Employment Cost Index and the Employee Benefits Survey. For more information, phone 202-691-6199 or visit http://stats.bls.gov/ncs/.

Other

Association for Library and Information Science Education. *ALISE Statistical Report and Database.* TN: ALISE, 1980-. Updated annually.

Average and median salaries for faculty and administrators in ALISE member schools are provided in this annual report by sex, rank and term of appointment.

Back issues (1981–) of the report are available from ALISE, 1009 Commerce Park Dr., #150, PO Box 4219, Oak Ridge, TN 37831-4219, 865-481-0155, (fax) 865-425-0155. The surveys from 1997 to 2005 are available for free from http://ils.unc.edu/ALISE/. This annual report is published in the summer.

College and University Professional Association for Human Resources. *National Faculty Salary Survey by Discipline and Rank in Four-Year Colleges and Universities.* Knoxville, TN: CUPA-HR. Updated annually.

Annual surveys collect data for faculty ranks in disciplines and major fields. Communications, Communication Technologies, Computer Information Sciences and Library Sciences are included. The listings are for those who teach in library science programs, not those who hold faculty rank as academic librarians.

For the print edition the cost ranges from $160 to $320; for Data on Demand (online access), from $500 to $1000. Contact

CUPA-HR, Tyson Place, 2607 Kingston Pike, Suite 250, Knoxville, TN 37919, 865-637-7673, (fax) 865-637-7674, http://www.cupahr.org/surveys/files/salary0708/SalSrvy08%20Order%20Form_4.30.08.doc.

Griffiths, José-Marie. *Future of Librarians in the Workforce.*

This two-year study (2005–2007) will identify the nature of anticipated labor shortages in the library and information science (LIS) field over the next decade; assess the number and types of library and information science jobs that will become available in the U.S. either through retirement or new job creation; determine the skills that will be required to fill such vacancies; and recommend effective approaches to recruiting and retaining workers to fill them. The study is led by Dr. José-Marie Griffiths, Dean of the School of Information and Library Science at the University of North Carolina at Chapel Hill and includes researchers from the University of Pittsburgh, Syracuse University, the Special Libraries Association (SLA), the Association of Research Libraries (ARL) and the American Society for Information Science & Technology (ASIS&T). More information is available at http://libraryworkforce.org.

French, Jennifer. 2006. *Fast Facts: Salaries of Librarians and Other Professionals Working in Libraries.* ED3/110.10/No. 238. Denver, CO: Library Research Service.

Fast Facts documents the pay distinctions between librarians' salaries in Colorado and other professions' salaries in the state. As well, the report compares all of the professional salaries in Colorado to national averages. The report is available at http://www.lrs.org/documents/fastfacts/238_BLS_lib_salaries.pdf.

"Placements and Salaries." *Library Journal.* Updated annually.

An annual survey since 1951 of ALA-accredited library and information studies education programs (usually published in the October 15 issue of *Library Journal* with data from previous calendar year). For each reporting school, the low, high, average and median salaries are reported for men, women and total placements. This information is also provided for five regions of the U.S. An additional table shows the distribution of high, low, average and median salaries by type of library for men, women and total placements. The current report is available at http://www.libraryjournal.com/article/CA6490671.html.

Employee Benefits

Although some states collect data on employee benefits, little information is collected on a regional or national level on a regular basis for library workers. The last report on Employee Benefits conducted by the American Library Association was in the *Librarian Salary Survey* supplemental questions from 2003. The report may be found on the ALA Office for Research and Statistics Web site at http://www.ala.org/ala/ors/reports/employeebenefits.htm.

Appendix D. Nonbinding Minimum Salary for Professional Librarians

ENDORSEMENT OF A NONBINDING MINIMUM SALARY FOR PROFESSIONAL LIBRARIANS

WHEREAS, The among the stated goals of the Allied Professional Association is "Direct support of comparable worth and pay equity initiatives, and other activities designed to improve the salaries and status of librarians and other library workers;"[1] and

WHEREAS, The Mean Librarian Salary in 2006 was $56,259;[2] and

WHEREAS, Over three-quarters of respondent library workers support the establishment of salary minimums for librarians, with the commonest salary figure cited being $40,000;[3] and

WHEREAS, The National Education Association has established a minimum salary of at least $40,000 for public school teachers, professionals whose qualifications closely mirror those of librarians,[4] now, be it

RESOLVED, that the American Library Association-Allied Professional Association endorses a minimum salary for professional librarians of not less than $40,000 per year; and, be it further

RESOLVED, that the details of this endorsement shall be published and otherwise disseminated by the Director of the ALA Allied Professional Association as appropriate.

Mover: Michael McGrorty, Councilor at Large
Seconder: Rob Banks, Kansas Chapter Councilor

Council Actions

During the American Library Association 2007 Midwinter Meeting in Seattle, WA, on January 22, 2007, the ALA-APA Council took the following actions:

Voted, To adopt APACD #15, Endorsement of a Nonbinding Minimum Salary for Professional Librarians.

---

1. See http://www.ala-apa.org/about/about.html
2. See "Librarian Salary Survey Reports Mean Librarian Salary Up More Than 4% to $56,259 in 2006" available at http://www.ala-apa.org/newsletter/vol3no11/salaries.htm
3. As found in the attached Survey.
4. See *Professional Pay: about NEA's Salary Initiative* at http://www.nea.org/pay/about.html

Appendix E. Endorsement of a Living Wage for All Library Employees and a Minimum Salary for Professional Librarians

APACD #8.2
2007-2008

ENDORSEMENT OF A LIVING WAGE FOR ALL LIBRARY EMPLOYEES AND A MINIMUM SALARY FOR PROFESSIONAL LIBRARIANS

WHEREAS, the American Library Association-Allied Professional Association (ALA-APA) Council, at its January 2007 Midwinter Meeting, adopted a resolution entitled "Endorsement of a Nonbinding Minimum Salary for Professional Librarians;" and

WHEREAS, the resolution resulted in a non-binding endorsement of a "minimum salary for professional librarians of not less than $40,000 per year;" which, adjusted for inflation now amounts to $41,680, and

WHEREAS, the ALA-APA Standing Committee on the Salaries and Status of Library Workers is charged "to guide ALA-APA activities in support of better salaries, comparable worth, pay equity, and similar programs related to the status of librarians and other library workers;" and

WHEREAS, the aforementioned Standing Committee sees the need to strengthen ALA-APA's position with regard to wages and salaries for all library employees, and with regard to variable costs of living over time and across geographical locations; and

WHEREAS, a living wage is defined as "net" or "take home" pay earned during a full-time workweek, not to exceed forty (40) hours per week. A living wage provides for the basic needs (housing, energy, nutrition, clothing, healthcare, education, childcare, transportation, and savings) of an average family unit; and

WHEREAS, the family of four Federal poverty guideline for 2008 is $21,200, a recommended minimum hourly wage of $10.20 is necessary for a full-time, year-round worker to exceed the poverty guideline and sustain a basic living; and

WHEREAS, the United States Bureau of Labor Statistics publishes the All-Urban Consumer Price Index (CPI), the standard measure for inflation of goods and services, which is adjusted monthly to reflect price inflation; now, be it

RESOLVED, that the American Library Association- Allied Professional Association endorses a minimum entry-level salary for professional librarians of $41,680 that is adjusted annually according to the latest cost of living index/CPI data; and, be it further

RESOLVED, that in recognition of the skills and competencies required of all library workers, the American Library Association-Allied Professional Association endorses a minimum wage for all library workers of at least $13.00 per hour, to be adjusted annually in relation to the Federal poverty guidelines."

---

1. See http://www.ala-apa.org/about/about.html
2. See "Librarian Salary Survey Reports Mean Librarian Salary Up More Than 4% to $56,259 in 2006" available at http://www.ala-apa.org/newsletter/vol3no11/salaries.htm
3. As found in the attached Survey.
4. See *Professional Pay: about NEA's Salary Initiative* at http://www.nea.org/pay/about.html